UNSETTLED

Graham Walker

UNSETTLED

In a hole. Climbed a mountain.
The life of a Big Issue man

Graham Walker

Illustrated by
Pete the Brush

Contents

Graham by Rose Tippin • 5
Introduction • 6

Section One
VERY COLD. GALE FORCE WINDS. POSSIBLE STRUCTURAL DAMAGE
Chapter 1 **Home sweet home** • 10
Chapter 2 **The great escape** • 16
Chapter 3 **Adulthood** • 27

Section Two
**A DEEP DEPRESSION BRINGING TORRENTIAL DOWNPOURS
AND LOCALISED FLOODING**
Chapter 1 **The longest night** • 34

Section Three
**LONG SUNNY PERIODS. CHANCE OF THE
OCCASIONAL HEAVY SHOWER**
Chapter 1 **Moving on** • 44
Chapter 2 **The pitch, postie and the public** • 51
Chapter 3 **Religion** • 63
Chapter 4 **Moving in** • 68
Chapter 5 **Out to lunch** • 77
Chapter 6 **Ripples** • 83
Chapter 7 **Friends** • 90
Chapter 8 **Out of the blue** • 103
Chapter 9 **Outlook bright** • 107

Published 2007 by Tangent Books
3 Monmouth Place
Bath BA1 2AT
Tel: 01225 463983
www.tangentbooks.co.uk

Publisher: Richard Jones

Production: Richard Jones, Anne Smith, Steve Faragher

Design: Joe Burt, Trevor Wyatt

Cover photography: Mark Simmons
0117 914 0999 · www.marksimmonsphotography.co.uk

From Graham. With much love.
To friends. Those I've lost, those I've found. To my children, Leanne and Andrew.
To the rest of my family, Keith, Gillian and Trevor. To my brother Geoff. To Jennie.
To Marc Leverton. To Kev the Hat for introducing me to music, life. To Slate Lady
for introducing me to style. To Pete the Brush and his magic pencil, Harberton
Arts Workshop. To Pip for her unfailing friendship. Finally, to anyone I've hacked
off, to anyone that didn't quite get it. I do apologise. I didn't mean to offend.

'Graham'
By Rose Tippin
(A Big Issue customer, a friend)

Graham takes. As a Big Issue man, he takes more in one day than you or I would take in a week, a month, or maybe even a year. He takes peoples' fears, stresses, anger, their compassion, friendship, laughter, cares, worries, their dislike and bigotry. He 'receives' all these emotions, digests them and carries them with him.

I admire Graham for his genuineness, his lack of ego, his acceptance of all who come his way. To accept and not judge, assume or criticise. I'd like to think that maybe some of his goodness has rubbed off on all who have met and talked with him.

Graham gives. As a Big Issue man he has raised over £50,000 in cash and gifts for local charities. As a Big Issue man Graham was honoured by being chosen as Barnstaple's citizen of the year. As a Big Issue man Graham makes a huge impact on all the towns he visits and indeed the people he meets.

In each copy of the Issue he sells, Graham writes an 'insert'. These take the form of stories, anecdotes, poems… whatever. We have heard, through his inserts, the tales of his travels, the incidents he recalls reducing us to tears and/or laughter. Graham has so many tales to tell.

He is a worrier though. Usually about letting people down, about moving to a new pitch in a new town, about whether people will like him. He needn't worry. From my experience and watching people's reactions to Graham, he should never worry

I'm so glad Graham has put together this book. I'm proud to call him my friend - no matter where he goes.

Introduction

L ife randomly deals everyone their own straw and I suppose, in the scheme of things, I was dealt a pathetically short one. But I have always conveyed and grasped hold of the positive. There are many out there whose straws are much shorter.

When putting this little book together, I asked my brother and sister for their recollections of childhood. I was amazed at how little I knew of their experiences. I was amazed at how horrific those experiences were. My sister, between the ages of six and ten, was 'rented out'. And my brother, a vulnerable child in a vulnerable environment, was abused by the very people who were placed in a position to help and care for him. The reconstructed pain of researching and revealing in detail these and many other disturbing events would be too painful for me, too tortuous for them.

So this, my route to homelessness, is a brief overview of how it actually was. What it is not, is a tale of self pity. What it is not, is an 'if only'. What it is, is one example, a single offering that may explain why some people struggle, why some disappear and why I believe I was destined to, one day, arrive on the streets.

But what does homeless mean to you? In simple terms, it of course means without a home. But what constitutes a home? OK, a guy sleeping rough, perhaps for no reason other than circumstance – circumstance that can visit anyone – no friends, no family, locked firmly into the mind-numbing effect of drink or drugs in order to eke out yet one more miserable day. Yes, he would fit 'comfortably' in the centre of the homeless spectrum. But there are many behind closed doors whose position, whilst perhaps not life threatening, is nonetheless as miserable, as desperate and as homeless as homeless gets.

The guy sleeping rough is visible. We know he's there. He may prick our conscience. He may, in some, spark disgust. But we are aware of his position. And whilst he may not have the strength or will to help himself, due to his visibility, there's a hope and possibility that in some form, help might come to him.

The invisible homeless, those behind their closed doors, whilst not being condemned by passers-by, will rarely receive any offer of help. Nobody knows they are there. We are oblivious to their situation.

'Going home' for some, is not that at all. It's going back to a house, flat, or bedsit, that's often papered in misery, fear, loneliness. Myself, my brothers and sister were, on the surface, 'housed'. But each and every one of us spent a childhood that was homeless!

'Home' is a much maligned word; dwelling place, house, base. These are all just one single constituent in the equation that makes a home. It's also somewhere you look forward to getting back to. A haven. Somewhere you feel comfortable, secure, snug.

The lonely guy who lives in some seedy bedsit having lived most of his life in institutions, until 'care in the community' knocked him sideways. Homeless! The widow next door, alone, struck with grief beyond belief for the man that's no longer there. Her long days filled staring through a window at a world she's afraid to re-enter. Homeless! The guy whose flat's a cesspit full of take-away corpses and empty vodka bottle dreams. Homeless! The young girl who lives in middle-class suburbia, roaring fire, over-stacked fridge, holidays abroad and a father who visits her bedroom late at night. Homeless!

How much would that young girl envy the girl with traveller parents, living in the back of a bus, itinerant, and to others, homeless, but living a life that is mouth-wateringly rich in guidance, security, happiness and love.

Home, a snug, safe and much maligned word. Home, more a state of mind than one of being.

Graham Walker, September 2007

VERY COLD.
GALE FORCE
WINDS.
POSSIBLE
STRUCTURAL
DAMAGE.

Chapter 1
Home sweet home

I was born into a family of five children, a variety of dogs, two cats, one habitually violent father and a correspondingly nervous and frail mother. My father was a rag and bone man, my mother a 'gofer'. She seemed to spend her entire life running errands for neighbours, leaving little time to look after the home, or us. She would sacrifice anything and everything to help or please others. Often at the expense of her own children.

We lived on a huge council estate in the north of Bristol. The home which should have contained love, guidance and security, instead held nothing more than violence, squalor and chaos. A house that was so filthy, council workers would refuse to enter to carry out remedial work, so filthy that going to bed involved entering a room with no light bulb, trying to visualise where the twenty or so dog faeces lay, before reaching a mattress placed on the floor in the corner. A home so bad that whenever the electricity ran out, as seven and eight year olds we were often sent out to knock on neighbours' doors to beg for money. If this failed, as it usually did, I would be despatched with an old halfpenny to file it down on the back doorstep until it reached a size that would fool the meter into believing it was a shilling. A home so sad that at pub closing time, we were occasionally hoisted out of bed by our mother. All five of us, then aged between 5 and 14, huddled behind the front door waiting for our father to drunkenly stumble in, then Gulliveresque-style, pin him to the floor whilst my mother bravely ransacked his pockets for money to buy food. Bravely, because she knew that if the following day, he managed to recall the previous evening, there would be a heavy price to pay. A price that would often cost almost everything breakable in the home. Including bones.

It was a home so sad that we never once invited friends back, not only due to the environment in which we lived, but also because we didn't really have friends.

When I was eight years old, my father and his fists were forced to leave the home 'for good'. Surprisingly, other than the random flashes of violence, home life remained pretty much the same. The difference it made to my mother was that she wasn't continually beaten and she also had extra time to run even more errands for neighbours. For us, little else changed. Still manic, still dysfunctional, still filing down halfpennies.

Even at this early stage in my life, I was aware that the environment we lived in was not like any other I'd witnessed. I was aware that I lived with a deep sense of shame. If my brothers and I were out playing in the street and we saw a school 'mate' walking towards us, we would distance ourselves from the house, wanting as few people as possible to know the hovel we lived in. When, on the odd occasion I was driven home by a school mate's parent, I would pretend I lived in the next door neighbour's house. I would enter their gate, wave goodbye, then walk around to the back of the house before clambering over the adjoining hedgerow in order to get home.

I was not yet aware though, of the psychological damage that each of us was now living with. Damage that remains to this day. Our social, interactive skills, through the environment in which we lived, were as absent as the love we so desperately needed. For me, with little other influence, I seemed to adopt my mother's character; weak, eager to please, desperate to be liked, but armed only with a feeling of utter inferiority. I lived in a world where I didn't really belong. I felt totally alien to all around me. Yes, the damage, whilst not yet apparent to me, was visible for all to see. On one occasion, sat in my classroom, I was desperate to go to the toilet. I tried to hold on but I couldn't, so I shit myself. I just didn't have the confidence to interrupt class. Instead I took the easier option; weeks of humiliation and derision from my school mates.

There are many memories that now indicate how that damage was delivered. None more significant than when my mother went away for a day trip. My sister and I, then aged 9 and 11, had a cunning plan. A plan beyond our years. A plan we'd put together over a week earlier when our mum told us of her trip. As soon as she was out of the door, the plan kicked into life. We were doing 'changing rooms'. The front room, being the place where we spent most of the time, was consequently the room that was the filthiest. The corners of the room housed mounds of dog crap that were simply covered up with old newspapers. It was cluttered with the debris of how we lived. Plates of half-eaten meals that had now evolved into lumps of furry mould, months of discarded newspapers, cans and bottles. Every shelf, every conceivable space was piled high with dust-layered rubbish. The linoleum floor, barely visible through the layer of grime that had built up over the years, now only matched the curtains that had long ago surrendered their pattern to the filthy hands that opened and closed them. And all this immersed in the stench that our nostrils were now almost immune to.

We set about our task. Well it was hardly a task. We'd been waiting for this moment for over a week. Now Mum had gone, that moment had arrived. We couldn't wait to get started. We couldn't wait to see our Mum's face when she returned home.

We had, over the course of the previous week, made certain preparations for the job in hand. One being the systematic lightening of Mum's purse by the odd coin. This, combined with the few coppers we'd saved from running neighbour's errands, gave us more than enough for the cleaning materials we needed. We'd also acquired, from the church jumble sale, two sets of curtains, nets and a large rug that we had stashed in a cupboard. We were ready to go.

For the next eight hours we had an absolute ball. My sister and I, working in total sync. With unbounded enthusiasm we cleared the room of over twenty bags of rubbish. With unbounded enthusiasm we cleared up the dog mess, scrubbed the floor, cleaned the windows. We washed skirting boards, doors. We scraped the mould from plates. We cleaned and polished anything and everything. With the room now cleared, the heavy sofa and chairs, normally confined to a small space next to the fire grate, were able to be shifted back, allowing us to lay the large rug that we'd bought. We hung the curtains and the nets. We replaced the ornaments and pictures. Yes, we did all of this with unbounded enthusiasm. The whole process was a most wonderful, happy and emotional experience. An experience, for both of us that was as memorable as it was rewarding. An experience that was peppered with many laughs, tears and hugs. My sister and I bonded that day. Two children with a common goal. Two children, not just thrilled by their own personal experience, but also each other's.

We stood back against the wall, surveying the panoramic fruits of our labours. It was beautiful. Absolutely beautiful. And we cried. I remember the sun shining through the snow white net curtains. It felt as though it had come to visit us and our room personally, glazing the whole space with a freshness and a warmth, pouring praise over what we'd achieved. There was just one thing left to do. I found a large piece of cardboard and in felt pen wrote on it, in huge black letters, 'OURS IS A NICE HOUSE, OURS

IS!' In almost ceremonial fashion, we together, placed this on the mantelpiece. And then we cried again. Our unbounded enthusiasm was now replaced with almost uncontrollable excitement and anticipation. It was 4.30pm. Mum was due back in half an hour.

Trevor, our six-year-old brother, kept watch for Mum at the garden gate, whilst we kept ourselves busy, adjusting curtains, straightening straight pictures, repolishing already repolished surfaces. And then came the call. "She's coming!" Hardly able to contain ourselves, we sat on the edge of the sofa. As difficult as it was, trying to act as nonchalant as possible. And then Mum walked in!

She entered the room, walked across the polished lino, stood on our new rug, threw her bags on the floor, then fell back into the chair that was now free from clutter. "Oh I'm shattered," she said. "Put the kettle on Gill. I could murder a cup of tea." Gill, paused, then almost in wretched defeat, strode slowly to the kitchen. I could hear her sobs. I ran out of the room, flung open the front door and sped up the street. I was utterly destroyed. Of course, I should have stayed with Gill. If ever there was a time we needed each other, if ever there was a time she needed me, that time was now. But it was difficult enough dealing with my own pain. I couldn't face anyone. Being older, I also felt overwhelmingly guilty over what my sister was now going through. What the hell was I thinking of? Never once had, or could our Mum show us any affection. No hugs. No kisses. No sleep-inducing stories. No approving nods, encouraging smiles. Never an acknowledgement. Never a thank you. I suppose I felt in some way, she would now have no choice in acknowledging what we'd done. No choice in thanking us. I was devastatingly wrong. My mum never did mention the front room. And neither did we. Not even between ourselves. Within three months, the front room had almost returned to its original state. It was like nothing had happened. But it had!

After my father had left, my mum did little in the way of finding a replacement. During the day running errands, the evenings spent sat on the edge of her chair, dangerously close to the coal fire, with a crossword book in her hand and her legs splayed, gleaning as much heat as possible. The constant heat producing large red rings all over her legs. Whilst we children usually formed a huddle on the sofa, covered in the coats that would at bedtime, substitute for blankets. Then one evening, Mum abandoned forever her crossword book, the coal fire and the edge of her seat, to take up a new position. A position right next to the window that

looked out onto the road. A position she would spend many evenings in, head poking through the net curtains, awaiting the arrival of an 'uncle'. Approaching headlights, the sound of a horn, and she was off! Yes, it seemed to take an age for my mother to embrace her new-found freedom but once she did… she did! Most evenings a random uncle would whisk our Mum away. Uncles identifiable only by the tone of their car horn. So most evenings we were left to fend for ourselves, armed with her departing words, "be good or you won't get any chips."

My brother Keith was two years older than me. Although good friends now, at the time we didn't get on. Consequently, while Mum was out, we'd often get involved in violent brawls. Although Keith was once hospitalised over one of these fights, he did, on the whole, get the better of me. So by 9pm I would often be found sat out on the front doorstep sometimes waiting for hours for Mum to come home. Distressed and crying, I would try desperately to eke out my tears until she arrived back so she could witness the extent of my trauma.

On her return late in the evening, we would all be rewarded with the luxury of a bag of chips and a bottle of lemonade, purchased from the rewards of her evenings out. Then aged 5, 9, 11 and 13 – my oldest brother Geoff, usually out doing his own socialising – we took fending for ourselves to a different level. One example of whiling the night away was playing war games. Quite simply it involved plucking clumps of grass and mud from the garden and, on the linoleum floor in the front room, creating a kind of landscape. Hills, fields, trenches etc. Then, igniting a few strategically placed firelighters that would act as camp fires, we would set fire to old dolls and other plastic toys, dripping molten bombs on the soldiers below.

Yes, this was an environment that, looking back, we were physically fortunate to survive. The act of bringing us up, I believe, was for my mum a chore. She just wasn't equipped. Most of her life was full of abuse. What little love she'd received she needed for herself. Unfortunately, as a child, I didn't recognise that. As an adult, I do. But whilst now I understand, it doesn't, and never can, erase the experiences and lifelong symptoms of a damaged childhood. It can never erase a childhood devoid. A childhood devoid of positive experiences. A childhood devoid of love.

But times they were a changin'. Whilst it wasn't going to get better, it was certainly going to get different!

Chapter 2
The great escape

Now aged 12, my brother and I rarely attended school. School was now for me, a dreaded chore. Lacking social skills, the only 'friends' I had were those I would entertain by being rebellious and disruptive. Smashing windows, swearing at staff, whatever! Even then the friendships were short-lived. So I'd always have to keep 'topping up'. It was my one and only ticket into the group. My one and only desperate ticket to belong. Mum herself, most of the time, didn't seem bothered whether we attended school or not. So we didn't. It was for this reason that my mother, brother and I were summoned before the family court. I remember feeling excited during the journey there. Being driven in our social worker's posh car evoked a sense of adventure, a day out of the norm. These feelings were immediately crushed as we were ushered to our seats in the wood-panelled courtroom. I looked up to face the panel of 'judges' and suddenly felt, as a 12 year old, totally overwhelmed, terrified. And then, court was in session.

After all the evidence was heard, after deliberation, the judges suggested to my mother that: "It might be in the boys' best interest to spend the rest of their childhood in a home." My mother, trembling, staring fixedly at the floor, muttered "Yes." I looked at her. What the hell was going on? Her stare remained fixed downwards. In retrospect, I know exactly what was going on. OK we were, all of her children, a burden to her. But sat in the courtroom, she was as overwhelmed as we were. The judge made a suggestion. Our mother was too weak to counter that suggestion. The poor thing just wanted to please! We never returned home that day and that would be the last time we would see or hear from our mother for months.

My brother and I never spoke a word as we were driven to the children's home. My head was reeling, everything was happening so fast. I looked across at him. He was two years older than me and it was the first time I'd ever seen him cry, but not even he could have imagined the seeds of trauma that had been planted this day. Neither of us could have envisaged the devastating events that would, especially for my brother, occur over the months and years ahead.

Vinney Green, the home that we'd been sent to, was, considering recent revelations, a typical 1960s–1970s children's home. By its very nature institutional, abusive in its manner and ultimately destructive towards its residents. Our daily routine was conducted with almost military precision. There were lots of rules and even more forms of punishment meted out to those who failed to obey. Punishments that I would later take advantage of.

It feels difficult to explain, and perhaps even more difficult to comprehend, the regime that existed at Vinney Green. To give an example of the consequences of breaking rules: talking in the dorm after lights out put you in serious risk of being dragged from your bed and made to stand for hours facing the wall in a darkened corridor. One brutal punishment I witnessed was when Tommy, a six or seven year old, was pushed to the ground and repeatedly kicked in the chest. His crime? He tried to run away, he tried to escape!

Vinney Green was a rambling old house with large hedged grounds. No-one was allowed outside these grounds, the exception being Sundays, when we were displayed before the local village as we paraded single-file to church. School itself consisted of two temporary buildings within the grounds, one for 4-10 year olds, one for 11-16 year olds. And so, this was Vinney Green – our new home!

It was a beautifully sunny day when Keith and I arrived. The children were having tea in the garden. We were introduced and I was offered a boiled egg sandwich. I humbly declined. "No thank you, I don't like boiled eggs." "You just eat it young man," insisted the huge woman overshadowing me. A combination of fear, natural politeness and the ever watchful eye of the 'giant' had me nibbling away at the edges of my sandwich, throwing it over the hedge when no-one was looking.

The initial numbness I'd felt on arrival quickly gave way to trepidation. I suddenly wanted home. I did, over the next few days, make a couple of friends and as the days grew into weeks, I became slowly accustomed to the regime (as I knew it), but then, without warning… CARROTS HAPPENED!

Now as a child, I used to loathe carrots. Well actually, I pretty much detested most vegetables, but carrots held a very special place in the pit of my stomach… or not! Having been weaned on a diet of chips, baked beans and chocolate cup cakes, I had never really grasped the toothsome and nutritional qualities that vegetables offered. I just hated them.

About a week or so after our arrival, sitting for dinner, the plate was thrust in front of me. Pie, potatoes and… CARROTS! AAGHH! Eating my meal, I tentatively nudged the carrots to form an orderly pile at the edge of my plate.

"Eat everything," a voice bellowed. I looked up to see one of the giants towering over me. "I can't," I replied. "Everything," she repeated in menacing tones. "I can't, I really can't," I insisted nervously. Negotiations over, led by my ear, my carrots and I were transported to the kitchen. I was placed at the end of a huge table where, under the supervision of the cook, I was told, "you don't leave here until your plate is clean, not until every carrot is eaten." So me, a giant and a plateful of carrots prepared to do battle.

I don't think the giant fully appreciated the size of the challenge ahead, not just for me, but for her as well. With various forms of enticement used, from disguising the carrots with heaps of tomato sauce, to holding my nose and trying to force the damn things down my throat. With over three hours passed, both drained by the ordeal, the struggle was finally over. The plate was clean. The carrots were gone! With a wearied, almost hollow air of victory, the giant ordered me to my bed. I walked off, limping slightly, as a pocketful of carrots slowly released their juices down my leg. Word of my hatred of the orange stuff soon got around and for me, the nickname of 'Carrot Face' was established.

Steve, a fellow dissident, a strapping 13 or 14 year old, was one of the kitchen assistants at Vinney Green. Well respected by all the other children, Steve became a close friend and ally who took me under his wing. I suppose it was inevitable. His nickname was 'Beefy'. His friendship gave me an immediate sense of security, a sense of importance, a feeling that everything would be OK. Feelings that I'd possibly never experienced in my whole life. But whilst Beefy could sort out most things, eliminating carrots from the menu was not part of his repertoire. A week or so after my first carrot encounter, Beefy approached me. "We got carrots on Friday." I froze. Only one option.

I had to escape!

Two days later, during our play session in the garden, whilst two 'inmates' kept one of the giants busy, Beefy and I ambled nonchalantly around the garden's perimeter. As I placed my foot in his cupped hands, I was launched in a flash, up and over the hedgerow, landing in a heap in

the adjoining field. I picked myself up and peered through the thicket. "Thanks mate," I whispered. I could just make out Beefy's face. He smiled. "Good luck, Carrot Face." I gulped, returned his smile and sped off.

The plan we'd thrashed out the previous day had worked to perfection, but this was where the plan ended. Where would I go? How would I get there? I ran and kept on running, simultaneously computing my options. Lost, afraid and very much alone. Whilst I didn't dare go back home, I had no choice but to go back to the estate where there were people I knew, people who might help.

The journey of some eight miles took the same amount of hours. It was dark when I arrived. Gill, my 10-year-old sister, spent most evenings with neighbours, the James family. There was a good chance my mother was out socialising. I just hoped Gill was there. Finding a telephone box, I reversed the charges and was put through to her. After explaining what I'd done, after her giggling fit had expired, we agreed to meet outside the house in ten minutes.

On my arrival, Gill and Mrs James produced an old Silver Cross pram. With me prised neatly inside, a blanket was tucked over me and I was wheeled almost nonchalantly past the police car parked outside my mum's, to the Johnson's. Now Mick Johnson was the local fence, a villain who was always sympathetic to those of us pursued by the constabulary. I was ushered into the house and ordered to hide in the attic until the police were gone. Sitting alone in the darkness, I imagined what it would be like to spend the rest of my life on the run. I certainly didn't envisage ever going back to Vinney Green.

For the next few days, I lived as part of the Johnson household, never daring to venture out. Then, with increasing publicity over my disappearance, combined with the persistent police presence, Mick reluctantly decided (I suppose due to the fact that his home was stacked floor to ceiling with stolen goods) that I'd become too hot to handle. With no other alternative, I asked Mick to telephone Mr Lancaster, my social worker. It was arranged that I meet him at the end of the street. Though I'd only met Mr Lancaster a couple of times, he had revealed what I perceived to be a vein of compassion; he did seem to understand. As I sat in his car, Mr Lancaster listened intently as I spoke of Vinney Green, my reasons for running away, my hatred of carrots, the cruelty I'd encountered and how I could never ever return. As I sat sobbing, Mr Lancaster hugged me,

reassuring me that everything would be fine, then drove me back to Vinney Green, and, as punishment, a plateful of carrots.

I attempted escape on a number of occasions over the months ahead, all except one successful, but the giants were becoming more diligent. Escape was fast becoming impractical. There had to be a better way!

My new methods of carrot avoidance were many in number and seemed to grow more ingenious with every encounter. They included forcing myself to be sick at meal times (which, when faced with a pile of carrots, didn't require the greatest of effort), or taping a polythene bag to my chest, forking a carrot, lifting it to my lips then triggering the carrot's release down my shirt into the bag, the fork seamlessly continuing its journey into my mouth. I would then turn to face the giants, chewing, and indeed grimacing on imaginary carrots. They, in response, giving me that 'I knew you'd come round in the end' look.

Once, struggling to devise my next carrot caper, it was, if you like, handed to me on a plate! A cleaner at Vinney Green found a discarded apple core behind one of the cupboards in my dorm. As no-one owned up to stealing the apple from the orchard, we were punished en-masse. For the next two days every meal for our dormitory consisted of a plate of cooking apples. If, at the end of the meal, an apple was half eaten, it was left for us to finish at the next meal. When carrots next reared their ugly heads on the menu, I was in the orchard, perched precariously up a tree, diligently waiting with my stash of apples. I jumped down just as one of the giants passed. NABBED! So, two days of cooking apples and another carrot-free day. You see, the giants were indisputably big, but they weren't altogether clever. They would in time, always discover what I was up to, but I would always think of a new scam, always one step ahead.

My only respite from the rigours of 'childcare' was my involvement in a project where people living in rural areas would give annual holidays to children from deprived backgrounds. This would be my fourth visit to Mr and Mrs Rudd on their farm in Dorset. It was always a magical experience, and since moving into Vinney Green, an oasis in my world of institution.

As I sat in the dormitory, a housemaster, Mr Green, entered and placed on my bed a bundle of clothes for my stay. As he left, I stared, mesmerised, as it lay atop the pile of clothing I'd been issued. It was still in its packaging. It was brand spanking new. It was the most wondrous black cotton shirt. In all my 12 years, this was the first new item of clothing I'd ever had. An irony considering my father had spent most his life in the rag trade, albeit at the lower end of the profession.

My dad, as a rag and bone man, spent his working days knocking on doors, exchanging bits of tat for bundles of old clothes that he could weigh in for cash. As a six year old I would often accompany him on his rounds, sitting on the back of his cart whilst he went about his business.

On returning home, we would all place the days 'takings' on the front room floor to form a large mound. We'd sit down, encircling it like boy cubs around a campfire, unable to touch until my father had first checked every single pocket for cash or anything else of value. Only then were we allowed to rummage. Each single item we chose had to be swapped, one for one, with clothes picked from previous piles. Sometimes we exchanged the very clothes we were wearing for cleaner, smarter ones.

"Transport's here." Mr Green yelled. I quickly packed my bag, ran out to the waiting car and was whisked away.

Arriving at the farm was, to me, like entering another world. A world devoid of emotional and physical grime, devoid of illogical rules and punishment. It's not that I was envious of it, but it was so far removed from the reality of my own world that it did highlight to dramatic effect how very grim my own world was.

After an emotional welcome I was shown to my room and left to unpack. I opened my bag and there it was. My beautiful black shirt. Lifting it out, I gently removed its cellophane packaging. The smell that met me is, 35 years later, as tangible now as it was then. I held it there, carefully removing its many pins and clips, its strangely shaped bits of card, its tags and tissue. This was clearly a very important shirt. I held it aloft. It was as black as the blackest coal.

White stitching neatly traced along each and every seam, pearlised buttons pinning back its collar. There were even buttons at the ends of its short sleeves, serving no purpose whatsoever but that's how important my shirt was. It wrapped itself around my face. I clung to it as I'd clung to nothing before; pulling away only for fear my tears might stain its fabric.

As always, my holiday was an amazingly powerful week, crammed full of adventure, underlined with a wonderful streak of freedom. And with Mrs Rudd's wisdom, and washing machine, my shirt and I rarely parted company. And then it was all over.

Back at Vinney Green, I entered the clothing store. "Dirty clothes Walker," ordered the housemaster. I passed him my clothes, keeping hold of my shirt. "And the shirt Walker," he demanded. "But sir," I protested. "It was only washed and ironed this morning. Perhaps I could wear it tomorrow?" "Shirt Walker."

I handed him my shirt and I was devastated. Of course, I knew the rules. No one had any personal clothing. All 40 children were issued a random set of clothes each day from the clothing store. But you see I had this stupid notion that my black shirt would remain with me forever.

The next time I saw my shirt was when a lad was vomiting down it due to one of the giants forcing him to eat his food. On another occasion I witnessed some disrespectful kid shedding his nasal contents into its short sleeve.

Then it came back to me. Standing in the clothing store, picking up my day's clothing, there it was. I rushed to the dorm and let it smother my face. Its wondrous smell long gone, as were half of its pearlised buttons. A gash had rendered its pocket lank and useless. Its bright charcoal appearance now grey and deathly.

Standing alone behind the orchard during our morning play session, I gently placed my shirt on the small fire I'd made. It briefly disappeared from view as it was enveloped in smoke. Then, as the flames took hold, it reappeared, as black as the blackest coal. The last glimpse I had was of one of its sleeves with the button that served no purpose whatsoever, until it too was engulfed in flames.

"What do you mean it's gone!" demanded a giant. "How could you possibly lose it?" "I haven't lost it," I snapped. "It's gone, that's all." I offered no further explanation in exchange for a sound beating and an early bed. They wouldn't understand.

Vinney Green was the first port of call when children entered the 'care' system. They would stay there for up to six months until an assessment was carried out as to what long-term care was most appropriate – foster home, adoption or larger institution. Keith and I, its longest residents, had been there for over a year. I've always taken that to be some kind of compliment.

One morning we were summoned to the office. The office was almost exclusively a 'giant-only' zone. Children admitted only when a major development was occurring. As I stood to attention before the huge desk, the giant looked up and smiled. Yes, definitely a major development occurring. "We've found you a new home," he announced. I was numb. "And here are your potential foster parents." I hadn't realised there was anyone else in the room, until an elderly couple, sitting in the corner, suddenly stood up. They looked at us with smiley eyes and pitying faces. We appeared to be acceptable. I was numb again.

Three weeks later, Mr Lancaster would drive us to our new home. I tried to imagine life without Vinney Green. I should have felt elated. No more needing to run, perhaps no more carrots. I felt nothing. When we were due to leave, I had to be forced, screaming and kicking into Mr Lancaster's car. By the time we'd arrived at our new foster home, I realised that whilst it would take every ounce of resolve, I had to get back. I had to get back. Back to Vinney Green, back to the very place I'd spent so much energy escaping from, back to the carrots, the routine, the institution I'd grown so accustomed to that it was now seemingly impossible to escape. Yes, I had to get back! A week later I was returned to Vinney Green, deemed unsuitable for fostering. My fault then! Some six months later I did finally leave Vinney Green when I was sent to another home; Cornercroft. Where I would also be returning to mainstream education for the first time in over two years.

Cornercroft was a fairly new concept in the childcare industry. It was a 'Family Group Home'. So called, because the homes were designed to replicate a family environment. A home that consisted of eight children looked after by two live-in members of staff. The staff in question, the 'uncle' and 'aunt' as they were referred to, were John and Elaine. We hit it off instantly. Now aged 14, I was the oldest child in the home. This afforded me certain privileges such as getting up early to prepare breakfast and supervising the children when playing in the garden. To others, these might be more suitably labelled as chores. No, for me they were definitely privileges. I felt useful, wanted, needed!

Over the course of my stay at Cornercroft, my relationship with John and Elaine grew ever stronger. I now felt loved as well. In the evenings, after the other children were asleep, I would be allowed back up to watch TV or join them for an evening meal. I felt so comfortable with them. The relationship was something I had never experienced. I loved them dearly. I was no longer just a kid in a home. With John and Elaine I was also a part of a family. Even the new school I attended didn't hold as many demons as I'd imagined. Whilst at Vinney Green we all had equal status. We were all kids in a children's home. At my new school, I suddenly became 'the' kid from the children's home. I thought that might cause a few problems, but in general, no. I came with an air of mystique. Other kids were intrigued, inquisitive. OK, I still had to perform the odd misdemeanour to ensure my friends remained so. And even these were to a certain point, tolerated by the staff, because of my children's home status.

I'd been at Cornercroft for more than fifteen months now. Then one evening, sat watching TV with John and Elaine, they told me they had some news for me. "Elaine and I are leaving next week," said John. "What d'ya mean, leaving?" Then John explained that he and Elaine had bought a guest house in Cornwall and would be leaving the following Monday. "A bit quick," I protested in an almost nonchalant tone. "We've known for two weeks, but we found it difficult to tell you," said Elaine. Of course it was naïve of me to think they would take me with them. But that's what I thought. A desperate thought. When they left, not for the first time in my life, my whole world imploded.

The next 'aunty' and 'uncle' to arrive didn't come with names. They were just aunty and uncle. They were as far removed from John and Elaine as is possible. Just as my relationship with John and Elaine had blossomed, my relationship with 'aunty' and 'uncle' deteriorated to the point of deep resentment and hatred. My family had gone. I was back in a children's home again. I rebelled. For the next few months I spent most of my time in my bedroom, sometimes through choice, more often as a consequence of my behaviour, both at home and school. I decided to run away. And this time it was going to be forever.

Sat in my classroom, I told one of my schoolmates my secret plans. He in turn relayed the secret to his friend, who in turn… By the end of the day half the class knew. This actually turned out to be a good thing. The following Saturday, I and 15 classmates met in the nearby woods and constructed a makeshift tree house. It felt great. I was not only part of a group, I was an integral part. With a pact of secrecy and a rota system for who would bring me food, the tree house became my home. Every morning and evening four or five schoolmates would arrive with parcels of food and a chat. This was an adventure. Made even more so by the police interest. And not one of my mates revealed a thing. Then, ten days into my stint up the tree, my cover was blown. The local park warden had taken an acute interest in the groups of kids that talked to the tree in his park every day. He contacted the police.

I remained in Cornercroft for a further six months until I became 15. It was then that my headmaster, aunt and uncle decided that, due to my disruptive behaviour, any further education was pointless. I was to leave school. Consequently I would also have to leave Cornercroft for a new home. 'Uphill', a working boys' hostel.

Not long after arriving at Uphill, I was found a job in a warehouse. Now, the system in the working boys' hostel was simple. You handed your wage packet over, unopened. The hostel would take out money for your keep. You were given a small amount for pocket money. Hardly a system that enabled independent living. After some months, it was a system I decided to buck.

When we were first put into 'care', it was initially deemed that we remained there until we were 18, unless we joined the Services. So, at 17, I joined the Army! After a few months in the military I returned to my mother's house on a weekend pass. I hitchhiked the 300 miles from Catterick to Bristol. A task made a lot easier when wearing a military uniform. During my first night back at my mum's house, I was woken to be informed that my elder brother Geoff – as a child, my absolute soul mate, mentor, best friend – was very seriously ill after being involved in a road accident. He wasn't expected to survive. My brother died three days later. I was grief stricken. I telephoned the Army and was told I would have to return to base and apply for compassionate leave! I went AWOL and attended my brother's funeral. It was time, once again, to buck the system. Six months later, I walked away from the Army, one dear brother less and the words 'SERVICES NO LONGER REQUIRED' stamped heavily on my passbook.

THE BIG
ISSUE

ONE WEEK ONLY
BUY TEN GET
ONE FREE!

Chapter 3
Adulthood

A childhood free from the trimmings of guidance, love, security, discipline and indeed logic – the very ingredients that form the solid foundation that enables us to become confident, free-thinking, independent and functional adults – is a childhood lost. When those ingredients are missing, there is no foundation. And I believe that the one thing in common between a foundation created by a loving, nourished childhood and the lack of foundation from an abusive, loveless or in whatever way, damaging one is that, in general, they stay with you forever.

My younger years had now left me as a sort of amorphous blob, characterless, a lump of jelly. An imposter, if you like; formless, but able at will to take on a shape, a personality, that might make people like or even love me. For the next four years I wandered the country working in low-paid, low-skilled, live-in jobs in the catering industry. By the time I was 23, I'd had 23 jobs. All but two ending in me walking away, sleeping rough until I found the next one. Then I finally arrived at Butlins in Minehead, where I would work for two seasons as a waiter. The environment suited me. I felt at home. All my physical needs were catered for. We all had equal status. It was like a children's home for adults.

Whilst there, I became good friends with a fellow waiter, Terry. Together, we worked hard, and played even harder. Being Butlins, our job as waiters was not played out in the most refined of establishments. But together, we honed our work and leisure time to perfection. Two seasons working 50-hour weeks, two seasons of more than many one night stands, two seasons of non-stop drinking and socialising. Two seasons of frenzy. An experience that at the end, delivered a huge physical and emotional hangover. I was wiped out. I once again, returned to Bristol. Once again to my Mum's.

Six months later, I met Jenny, my first and only long-term girlfriend. After another six months we married and a year later we had a son, Andrew. For the next four years we were relatively happy. For the first time since living in Cornercroft with Elaine and John, I'd found stability; I felt secure, loved, confident. Qualities though that deserted me each time I left the house. At work, as in school, I would still need to be rebellious, still a misfit trying to buy my ticket to friendship, and although less frequent, still moving from job to job.

Jenny loved me, and I so much needed that love. But eventually it wouldn't be enough. It would never be enough. I would constantly need the whole world to tell me I was OK, to reassure me, to encourage me, constantly shoring up a foundation of sand. A foundation of sand that was now tentatively supporting bricks of adult experiences. Bricks that would eventually come crashing to the ground.

Although home at the time was my only haven, I started to spend less and less time there. Now more suited to the chaotic life I was creating for myself outside. Chaos that would often accompany me home. Over the next two years, the more chaotic my life became, the more my marriage disintegrated. I wasn't functioning as a husband, or indeed a parent. As with my mother, I had nothing to give. I just wasn't equipped for the role. Although grown up in years, I was an adult in waiting. An adult waiting for his childhood to happen. Then one evening, my marriage ended. My wife didn't come home. Jenny, chaos and ultimately guilt had been the only long-term constants in my life. And now Jenny was gone.

For the next four years, I, but mainly my sister, looked after my son. I went through another clutch of jobs and a number of affairs, one of which resulted in my lovely daughter Leanne. My life though was by now in meltdown, spinning faster and faster out of control.

At 35, I was now almost non-functional. My son returned to his mum. Now on my own, over the course of the next year, I slipped slowly into an all-consuming depression, spending weeks without contact with the outside world. Locked inside my flat. Locked inside my head. Knowing my life was an utter mess, but without the strength or ability to do anything about it. To outsiders, I was experiencing a few niggling problems. For myself, I was in an untenable, all-consuming, multi-coloured tragedy.

Sometime later, I was at a point where I couldn't carry on; didn't want to carry on. So I decided to kill myself. Stood loitering outside a local chemist, picking my moment, I burst into the store, strode confidently up to the counter, grabbed two packs of Paracetamol, and then just as abruptly walked out again.

Later that day, in response to a pathetically feeble suicide attempt (I'd better phone my sister and tell her I've taken some pills), I entered hospital for a couple of days and was then transferred to a psychiatric unit.

Three weeks later, I returned to my flat. Opening the door, I nonchalantly kicked the pile of unopened mail that had stood there for months. Walking through the flat, I glanced at the half-finished décor projects, started a year earlier in a week-long fit of enthusiasm and scanned the mouldy dishes that had lain there, as I had, for weeks, in a complete state of lethargy. And at that moment, I knew I had to leave.

For me, as I'm sure for many others, my 'leaving' was not a choice, not a conscious decision. It was something that was happening to me. An event over which I had no control. Walking away from one's life, some may judge a selfish, cowardly act. Not always so. Doting fathers, loving responsible mums, adoring children who just disappear, don't suddenly stop caring, don't consciously set out to leave in their wake, desolation, grief and, in some cases, a lifetime of 'not knowing'. Like me, I'm sure many that go missing are, at that moment, hanging onto life by a thread and the weight of even thinking about the trauma you've left behind could be devastating, for everyone!

I remember standing in the lounge. It was a bright, extraordinarily bright sunny morning. Looking out to the communal garden below, I watched as a neighbour playfully tossed his giggling child in the air. Turning, I strode around the flat, grabbed a few personal possessions, and walked out, leaving my disastrous past behind, knowing I would never return. I ran down the stairs, out into the sunshine. I was suddenly, totally, wonderfully overwhelmed. I walked briskly along the street, not knowing where I was going, or indeed what I would do when I got there. Nothing, absolutely nothing mattered.

I was free! Free from the stress, the depression, free from putting my hands over my ears when the doorbell rang, free from the guilt of unopened letters, free from answering awkward questions from friends and family.

I was suddenly and immediately, with absolutely no effort whatsoever... free, anonymous, a lifetimes' burdens lifted. I was free. I was alive. I WAS HOMELESS!

THE BIG
ISSUE

PLEASE QUEUE
IN AN ORDERLY
FASHION

UNSETTLED

A DEEP
DEPRESSION
BRINGING
TORRENTIAL
DOWNPOURS
AND
LOCALISED
FLOODING.

Chapter 1

The longest night

S o here I was, homeless. But within days my initial euphoria was disappearing at a rate faster than the few pounds in my pocket. The overwhelming relief of walking away from, for me, an impossible situation, made it far easier to accept and, indeed, embrace street culture. Made it easier to accept the violence and drugs. Made it easier to embrace the alcohol and deprivation. I was very soon an integrated member of the community. A comfortably numb experience, but later frustrating and seemingly impossible to escape.

I entered a whirlpool of madness that transported me to a depth, a darkness, that even now I find hard to believe exists. A place from which it took every ounce of resolve to escape, and at a time when it seemed the only thing left to lose was my mind.

ROLL UP ROLL UP

**Welcome to my world of madness,
step inside my mind.
Walk right through the swirling mist,
what wonders might you find?
Ignore the walls of darkness.
Walk past the roof of gloom.
And if you find you lose your way,
head for the 'living' room.
Admire the vibrant coloured hues
that occasionally appear,
and sit upon the ride of love
that takes away your fear.
Glance at the hall of mirrors
etched with acts of yesterday,
distorted now but closely, look,
they never go away.**

I hope you do enjoy your trip,
and when the ride is done,
if you saw the hurt, I'm sorry,
but I never promised fun.

It was Friday the 23rd of December. I needed help. I turned to the organisation synonymous with homelessness. I telephoned the Salvation Army in Bristol. The other end of the phone informed me they had vacancies. Thank God. "Can I move in this evening?" I asked. Naively thinking that me being homeless and the Salvation Army having spare beds, I'd be sorted! Not quite so it seemed. Because I wasn't claiming DSS at the time, the Army wasn't guaranteed its weekly rent in the form of housing benefit. So, if I wanted to book in, I would have to pay 'cash up front', until the benefits office re-opened after Christmas. I fumbled with the few coins in my pocket. Certainly not enough to purchase a room at the inn. Sufficient though to buy me a one way ticket to the forget zone. I hung up and headed for the nearest off licence.

I spent the next year on the streets, witnessing 'colleagues' lives being cut short by the side effects of alcohol, drugs, winter nights and suicide. I then started to distance myself from the main street community. From

experience, this community, at times, could be unpredictable, explosive, occasionally lethal. I needed to feel in control. Even if I was anything but. I just felt safer if I remained alone. By day, alone with only cheap sherry as my companion. By night, trawling the city for undiscovered shelter; derelict house, building site, whatever. Then early one morning, I awoke in a park. I was obviously cold, but there was no shivering, no discomfort. I just lay there. I could sense my whole being, both physically and spiritually, ebbing and flowing. In an almost hypnotic state, it felt like my strength was fading as fast as my will. I jumped up and let out a huge defiant, invigorating roar, then realised, whilst I still had sufficient strength, I had to move on. I had to start again, now, before the minute flicker of ambition died forever. Now, before I too became just one more wretched, soon-forgotten statistic.

The following night, a dangerously cold night, I went 'indoors'. The Bristol night shelter, an old warehouse accommodating 20 or 30 beds, whilst not the most prestigious of establishments, appeared a damn sight more attractive than sleeping outside to cope with the ravages of winter.

Stood outside the huge metal doors, I distanced myself from my fellow strugglers. These were regular shelter goers. A volatile mix of schizophrenics, alcoholics, heroin users, self harmers and teenage runaways. As the doors opened, people rushed to the corner of the shelter where volunteers doled out soup and bread. Some gathered in groups, shouting and drinking. Others sat eating what, for most, would be their only meal of the day. The 'cases' would sit alone on their beds waiting for the blankets to be doled out. The noise in the shelter was deafening. The atmosphere manic. The experience no less harrowing than the last time I'd succumbed to the 'luxury' of the night shelter.

At midnight, the lights went out, to be followed by a drunken orgy, slowly reducing in volume, as one by one, people slipped into unconsciousness.

In the adjacent bed lay a 17- or 18-year-old girl being entertained by the silhouettes of a couple of middle-aged Irish guys. Each vying for the girl's affection. Each armed with a dowry of a cheap bottle of sherry. I pulled the pillow over my head. Sleep constantly interrupted by the noise of a coughing fit, a nightmare-induced scream, a person relieving themselves in the urinal. Waking in the early hours, the lights came back on. I pulled out a book and, for a time, lost myself, whilst the rest of the warehouse slowly stirred. I looked across to see the young girl asleep. The two Irish guys reappeared. Nudging her awake, she slowly came round. They gently

lifted her head, offering a bottle of sherry to her young dry lips.

She obliged, slightly grimacing on the nectar she hoped would see her through another day.

I sat eagerly waiting for the doors to open. Reaching in my pocket, I pulled out and lit a cigarette. From the corner of my eye I noticed an old boy watching intently. I knew the script; I was just about to be tapped. He shuffled towards me, his urine-starched clothes and the accompanying stench slowly filling my space. "I'm off to Scotland in a minute." I looked up. "Oh great," I replied. "Yes, I've sold my house up there, I'm off to the solicitors to pick up my money… you couldn't spare a fag could you mate?" I obliged. "Yes, I'm going to buy a little place in Spain, can't stand these bloody winters no more." He pulled hard on his fag, soaking in sufficient nicotine to line his face with a pallor of satisfaction. He continued talking of his trip. As he spoke, I watched him. This was a real gent; he'd already given a performance that far outweighed the cost of a cigarette, but he carried on, lost in his dream.

He was interrupted by two other guys, one of whom slapped him smartly on the back. The old man jumped. "Come on Mickey, get your gear, Jim's got a double Giro. We're all meeting in the park for a swallow." Mickey's face lit up, then, turning to me, took on a pained expression. "I'll go tomorrow… yeah, tomorrow, bright and early!"

As the metal doors squealed slowly open, allowing sunlight to pierce the emotional blackness, I strode out. Out into the vividly bright open space of opportunity. Feeling, for the first time in a very long while, confident, optimistic about what might lay ahead. Three weeks later, I managed to secure a place in a men's hostel. A major step forward. The hostel was situated in Bristol's inner city area. A large Victorian building housing 40 to 50 residents. After booking in, I soon realised it wasn't quite the major step I'd first imagined. The hostel was equipped with a large communal kitchen, TV room and two large dormitories. These consisted of a long narrow corridor with twelve cubicles on either side. The cubicles, each having a lockable door, measured some 8' x 5'. They had no ceiling and were each separated only by a partition. It became apparent that valuables should never be left on the floor, as I found to my cost. Hands from adjoining cubicles often found their way under the partition, relieving you of anything within their grasp. The stench in the dormitories dictated that it was purely a 'sleep only' zone. If I was asked for a one word description of the hostel, it would be 'bedlam'.

Residents included newly-released prisoners, long-term homeless pensioners and men who were victims of 'care in the community', the innovative scheme that was introduced some time earlier. The innovative scheme that seemed to lack two essential ingredients: community, and of course, care. There was, indeed, a good level of staff support. But it was designed to get you a home, get you a job. It was in no way designed to, and in no way capable of, addressing the complex problems of its residents. One particular man who had severe mental health problems would often shave his head, hacking away at it with a razor until his whole scalp was covered in blood. Instead of the professional help he so desperately needed, he'd instead had two written warnings over his behaviour. A third would see him evicted, thrown out on to the streets. Another man I witnessed during my stay there was an exceedingly timid character in his early 30s. I never saw him once speak or interact with anyone. He would often be found at the sink in the communal kitchen, washing his utensils under the cold tap and then under the scalding hot one. And then his hands. Manically alternating between hot and cold then scrubbing them with a nail brush until they were red raw. A member of staff informed me his name was Mike. One day, I interrupted his painful ritual and spoke his name. For a split second, he turned to me revealing eyes containing nothing other than abject terror, then, just as quickly, he turned back to once again go about his business.

I'd been living in the hostel for two months now and during the past couple of weeks, two or three residents had been mugged after cashing their sickness benefit. A few days later, I overheard a conversation revealing that one of the residents in the hostel was passing information to his mate on the outside as to when an easy victim was due at the Post Office. So, all be it tentatively, I had a word. He told me to "fuck off". I reported it to a member of staff who appeared as nonchalant as she was powerless. As it was happening outside the confines of the hostel, she could do nothing. The following day, walking to the local homeless day centre, I was bustled down an alley. The knife put to my throat was accompanied by the words: "Mind your own fuckin' business!" Damn good advice. Advice though, if I were stronger, I should have dismissed. Two days later it was Mike's turn to be the victim. As you can imagine, he took it harder than most. He took his own life.

I left the hostel to lay low for a few days. I needed the time and the space to think what my next move might be. It didn't take much working out. For safety's sake, I had to leave the hostel. For sanity's sake, I had to leave Bristol.

IT'S BEDLAM

Some child today will be nurtured and cherished
Prepared for a life that is no doubt sun-kissed
Some child today will sit squat in a corner
Nursing the wounds from a well-planted fist

Someone today will arrive on the streets
For an age, the place they were destined to land
Someone today will condemn what they see
Cos it's easy to curse, not so, understand

Today, someone will enter this world
They'll open their eyes and cry
Today, someone will think time's on their side
Today, someone will die

Someone today won't smell the flowers
Too busy chasing the scent of the pound
Someone today will lie 'mongst the daisies
Lost in the wonder that lay all around

Someone today will work for a pittance
Producing such goods they could never afford
Someone today will have all they desire
Yet life still won't get to strike the right chord

Someone today will gamble a million
On the turn of a card or the roll of a dice
Someone today will die from starvation
For the sake of fresh water and a few grains of rice

Someone today will be sent off to war
To perform in a fight that will never be won

Someone today will pick up the 'phone
To discover they've seen the last of their son

Today, someone will think time's on their side
Today, someone will die
Today, someone will lie 'mongst the daisies
Lost as the world trundles by
Today, someone will question that world
And plead for the answer to why
Today, someone will enter the race
And see all the madness and mayhem apace
And with questioning eyes on an innocent face…
… today, someone will cry.

I returned to the hostel to retrieve my belongings and leave immediately. But it wasn't that easy. It seemed I would have to lose everything in order to find, and eventually walk, the road that would lead me to a better place. Arriving back at the hostel, I discovered that all my personal possessions kept in a couple of plastic bags, had been unwittingly cleared out as refuse. I now had nothing. No photographs, driving licence, no treasured letters, documents or mementoes. Nothing. I was devastated. I left the hostel and headed for Devon. The following day, I entered Plymouth with a couple of pounds, a carrier bag containing a change of clothing, and no past. Surely my whole past couldn't be obliterated purely by the loss of two plastic bags.

I still have two children; the real thing easily replaces photographs. I have friends I've made on the way. There are people whose lives I have touched and there are certainly those who have touched mine. I exist, even with no paper document to confirm that. My achievements remain just that, achievements, even if no record exists. But most importantly, I have my memories. Good or bad, they get me through. They make me smile, they make me laugh aloud, they sometimes make me cry, but for sure, they stay with me, always, giving me warmth, comfort, a sense of being.

Having no possessions was like losing my right hand. But my other 'hand' became stronger, more adept. My memories, through necessity, became more focused. My mind became the black plastic bags, holding my possessions, my life, which I can draw from whenever I need.

41

LONG SUNNY
PERIODS.
CHANCE OF
THE ODD
HEAVY
SHOWER.

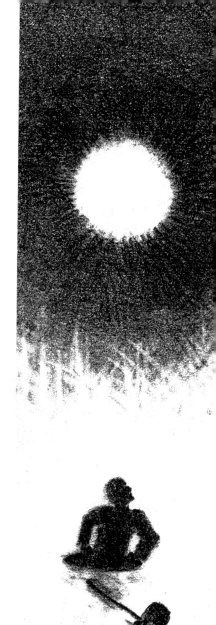

Chapter 1
Moving on

I arrived at Plymouth in late Spring. A new beginning? It certainly felt that way. If there was ever a Square One, this was it. Alone, no home, no friends, no possessions.

I acquired a sleeping bag and blankets from a local charity shop and found shelter in the form of an old Second World War gun turret that overlooked the River Tamar. The shelter was fairly well known among the homeless community so there were often visitors stopping for the occasional night. A regular visitor was Mark who, like me, had just arrived in Plymouth. Mark was 26 and had lived on the streets since he was 15. Although younger in years, he was far more astute than I, far more street wise. When walking around town, he was able to sniff out any opportunity that might lead to some food, drink or money.

After a couple of weeks, we entered the recycling industry, trawling around Plymouth collecting discarded cans. Mark was clearly well practised at this. Steel cans were worthless, only aluminium would do. Mark knew the difference just by identifying the brand. Coca Cola, yes. Tennents, yes. John Smiths, no. A recycled can was worth about 1.2p. A full day's work usually earned us a bite to eat, a bottle of drink and a good night's sleep.

One day, we were experiencing a bit of a can famine. Mark suggested we give the waste bins on Plymouth Hoe a try. It was a good move, the refuse collectors hadn't been around yet. The bins were brimming. Then Mark, on pulling a half full can of lager out of a bin, proceeded to drink it. "Someone might have pissed in that," I remarked. "Wouldn't be the first time," he replied. "But I'm gagging." So this was Square One. This was my new beginning.

Two days later, I resigned my post in the recycling trade and left the shelter to set up home a couple of miles away. That very evening I was joined by a young couple who were sleeping rough just around the corner from my shelter. We chatted and they kindly shared their food and drink with me. They told me that they sold The Big Issue in town and offered to accompany me to the office to get 'badged up'. The following day I took them up on their offer and was assigned the 'pitch' outside Boots in

Plymouth city centre. With ten free Issues to start me off, I nervously set up stall. Within a couple of hours I'd sold out. The £10 in my pocket felt like a million.

Over the next few weeks, I became a regular Issue seller. I soon made friends with a group of other sellers and was invited to move into the large shelter they were sharing on Plymouth Hoe. We became inseparable, always meeting up after work to discuss the day's events and share a bottle or two. Selling The Issue seemed to fit like a glove. Meeting and interacting with the public, socialising with friends. I felt at ease. For the first time in years, my life seemed to have some structure. My world, and indeed the world around me, seemed so much brighter.

Now I suppose if there is an obvious flaw in my already flawed character, it would be never learning from my mistakes. But it felt that now having found structure, now that my world was so much brighter, my times on the streets were behind me. So I moved into a hostel in Plymouth. Mistake! This was a huge, *Fawlty Towers* of a hostel. A hostel that relied on funding. Funding that relied on targets. And targets that relied on ticks! On paper they must have been one of the most achieving hostels in the country. In reality, anything but. During my short time within the confines of this hostel, I witnessed at least ten guys that were found 'permanent'

accommodation. Yes, permanent; seedy, private bedsits and shared houses. Some of these guys had major alcohol and drug problems, some of these guys had been homeless for more than 20 years. With the hostel providing no ongoing support, no further contact, I consequently witnessed at least ten guys back on the streets within weeks. Yes, another ten ticks, another ten paper successes.

On arriving, I was put through the induction process, then shown to my room, 'the drink tank'. This was a multiple occupancy room that housed those with severe alcohol problems. Although I was no longer alcohol or drug dependent, as a new resident it was deemed I was, until I demonstrated otherwise. Guilty until proven innocent!

The hostel was run almost as a military establishment. Being Plymouth, every room in the hostel was named after a ship; Raleigh, Invincible, Drake. Even the walls of the hostel were adorned with large black and white photographs showing troops of naval ratings doing synchronised exercise and drills. Supposedly to inject a sense of order into its residents. (I've always found sunflowers work best).

Anyway, three days in the 'drink tank', three days sober, I passed the test. I was promoted! Yes, due to proving myself, I was promoted to a room with only two beds. Better still, after another two weeks sober, I was promoted yet again. I was given my own room! There was only one rung of the ladder left, the room that was situated on the top floor of the hostel. A room that even had its own cooker and TV. A room where you were actually entrusted with your very own door key. The room, (sick bags ready) was called the 'Crows Nest'. I never quite made it there. My birthday happened!

Yes, it was the 24th of April, my birthday. My brother brought my son down to Plymouth. I was taken out for the day. A wonderful day, topped off with a wonderful celebratory meal washed down with a couple of glasses of wine. After a tearful goodbye, I returned to the hostel. I was let into my room and slept soundly on a pillow of sweet memories.

The following morning I went out for a walk with friends, returning to the hostel early afternoon. On being let into my room, I was aghast. I'd been robbed. All of my clothes and the few personal possessions I had were gone! A member of staff tried to calm me down, trying to assure me there must be an explanation. And indeed there was an explanation. Unbeknown to him, unbeknown to me, due to a member of staff having smelt alcohol on my breath the previous evening, whilst I was away, my clothes and possessions had been bundled into a bed sheet and dumped into a shared room. I'd been moved. I'd been demoted! I entered the room and just stared at this sheet topped with a knot. It suddenly became symbolic. A sheet that had been irreverently dumped on the floor. A sheet that contained my life. A sheet, a life that deserved respect. I immediately grabbed my life and we both walked away.

I remained in Plymouth for eighteen months, selling and socialising. But I was becoming increasingly frustrated. Frustrated at the daily pattern. Frustrated over the fact that the socialising was now starting to occupy more of the day than the selling. I was bored. For me, the party was over. I'd achieved so much here. I was stronger, rejuvenated, more able to cope. Qualities which, in turn, were leading to frustration. Qualities that were I to remain, could so easily be wiped out. Yes, for me, the party was definitely over. I needed more. It was time to move on.

Whilst my friends would always remain so, Plymouth, like Bristol, would from now on be solely a place to visit. I realised my role as a Big Issue vendor was one I still needed to play, but also one I needed to hone. A role that I needed to evolve into one that best suited my character. Above all, I needed to be independent. I needed to be in control.

That independence came in the form of the tent I purchased. It also gave me the opportunity to sell in smaller towns, towns that were far less impersonal. I then designed an 'A' board out of an old clothes airer and a roll of lining paper. A sign that displayed messages such as 'Please queue in an orderly fashion'. 'Buy ten, get one free'. The sign had a number of effects. Standing behind my sign gave me my own space. It slightly increased sales. More importantly, to the world around me, it turned me into a human being, approachable, someone who could read and write, someone who, given his situation, still maintained a sense of humour. I then started to include within my Issues' an insert, a photocopied anecdote or poem I'd written depicting my experiences as an Issue seller or a story from my past. These, unintentionally, acted as an ice breaker. If nothing else, people now knew my name. An important start to any relationship. In no time, my pitch not only became my place of work, conversing with customers and developing friendships also satisfied my social needs. But I still needed more. That 'more' was to happen in Totnes, Devon. Well it started surreal enough.

After buying my Issues in Plymouth, I ambled up to the railway station to catch the train to Totnes. The display monitors informed me there was an 11.10 to Glasgow. Alternatively, being in no particularly hurry, I could grab a cup of tea and catch the 11.52 to Paddington.

Stood pondering, an official marched up and enquired as to my destination and what train I was catching. Instinctively, I replied "the 11.10 to Totnes". "Oh dear, I'm terribly sorry," he said, "but that train has been cancelled and is now leaving from Exeter." "Oh dear," I replied, looking at my non-existent watch, as though reaching Totnes on time was a matter of life or death. "I do apologise sir, it's been an awful day, what with the Virgin breakdown and the signal failure at Truro and, ironically, I should have been on holiday this week but Shirley, that's my wife, well she…" I looked up to see his military frame slowly buckle. I interjected with a reassuring pat on his shoulder. He looked at me soulfully. I reciprocated with a slightly less firm but even more reassuring pat, along with a look that said 'it's going to be alright mate, together we're going to get through this.' With a grateful nod, he took a deep breath, pulled back his shoulders and invited me to follow him. Marching briskly across the concourse, with me in hot pursuit, respectfully trying to keep in step, I was invited to join a small group of people (all would-be 11.10ers). There was Steve and Sarah, a lovely couple from Ivybridge looking at engagement rings. John, job interview in Exeter and Emily, a frail, slightly confused old lady who I don't think was catching the train anyway.

After 20 minutes or so of acquainting myself with the group, we looked across to see Ernest, our official, fairly skipping across the station towards us. "You can all have taxis!" he proclaimed triumphantly, enthusiastically waving his arms in the air. Apparently, due to the cancellation, all passengers travelling between Plymouth and Exeter had been awarded free taxis. As I was the only one travelling to Totnes, I was offered the only cab on the rank outside. With hurried kisses, goodbyes and best wishes exchanged on engagement, job interview, Big Issue sales and Emily's sanity, I walked to my taxi.

With his air of officialdom now fully restored, Ernest opened the cab door and firmly shook my hand. I thanked him for all his help and climbed into the cab. As the taxi pulled away, I glanced back to see my new found chums waving goodbye, whilst Ernest stood upright, one hand held high in full military salute, his other draped lovingly over Emily's shoulder.

As tears welled in my eyes, I felt an overwhelming sense of loss when in truth, I should have been feeling a deep sense of guilt… I hadn't even bought a ticket!

Totnes, a wonderful town, was good. Good for me, good to me. It was exactly what I needed. Through my 'inserts' people got to know me. Within days my tent and I were safely ensconced in a customer's orchard. Within weeks it felt as though I'd been totally accepted as a member of the community. Eventually there wouldn't be a customer that wasn't also a friend. It felt so, so good. At last, I'd found the very thing I hadn't consciously set out to find, but the very thing I needed. A sense of belonging.

Then sat in my tent one evening, I pondered on how fortunate I was. I also pondered on the amazing support I'd received since my arrival. Then in a flash, my 'more' finally arrived. The 'more' that would meld all the wonderful events that had occurred since my arrival in Totnes, into one organic, amazing experience. I needed to give something back. I needed to do some fundraising.

Some of my new-found friends belonged to a group that raised money to bring children from Chernobyl over to England for respite holidays. The cost per child was £250. So that's the amount I decided to raise. To achieve my goal, I'd arranged to stay on my pitch, 24 hours a day for a whole week, asking the local community to sponsor me for my efforts.

At the start of the week, I was more terrified than nervous. Would people trust me, a Big Issue man? Would people trust me enough to hand their money over? For me, I was taking a huge risk. I could see it all falling apart. I had even made plans to move on to another town should that happen.

Within half an hour of starting my week's stint, my fears were proved unfounded. A man, a stranger, walked up, handed me an envelope, and without stopping, walked off again. The envelope contained £250 in cash.

For me, and I believe also for the town, it was a memorable week. A wonderfully fulfilling experience with a heart-stopping, roller-coaster of emotions. A week that raised a total of £2,400.

My Big Issue pitch suddenly seemed the perfect platform for fundraising. Successful perhaps because it was an anomaly. A Big Issue man raising money for others. Successful perhaps because I injected every ounce of energy into ensuring it was. Who knows? Stood on the streets, I became a visible focal point, a channel for other people's generosity and compassion. Two weeks later I left Totnes.

So, the pattern was set. I would enter a town. Anonymous. Through my 'inserts' people would get to know me, respect me. Relationships would form, friendships develop. I would slowly become a part of the community and people would start to trust me. When that trust reached a level that was actually tangible, I would embark on my next fundraising.

Throughout all my fundraising experiences, as much as the people and organisations need the money, I too need to raise the money. It supplies me with a sense of meaning. It quantifies my very existence (pure selfishness I tell you). Yes, the whole experience becomes a more organic one.

But as in Totnes, shortly afterwards I would leave. I'd get to a point, sometimes overnight, when I'd feel the challenge was over. I'd outstayed my welcome. My relationship with the community had reached its peak. It would from now on be simply a case of maintaining that relationship. Something I have never been good at. Something that carried with it the chance of me in some way destroying or, at the very least tarnishing, the very thing I'd spent so much energy in creating. I would desperately need, once again, anonymity; a fresh challenge, a new community. That may sound sad, perhaps negative. Leaving behind everything I'd spent months creating. It is, for me, always a huge wrench leaving a town, leaving behind friends and relationships. But my life now had meaning, substance, fulfilment. I had everything I needed. Respect, trust, love! The very things I'd missed out on as a child. My customers, if you like, became my family. The South West, my home.

I've at last found a sense of belonging.
It's taken an age to arrive.
For me it's the end of a tortuous journey,
one I thought I might never survive.
A sense of belonging's a wonderful thing,
not something you set out to achieve.
It sort of just happens,
and now that it has,
finally, I'm able to breathe.
So I'm here now 'for good',
though I still need to roam.
It's good to be here.
It's great to be home.

Chapter 2
The pitch, postie & the public

I t's a strange part of the process. Moving from a town, a community where I'm totally accepted, to then enter a town where I'm completely anonymous, where certain elements of the community treat me with disdain.

When moving 'home', when entering a new town, like everyone else, I have to undertake a few tasks before settling in. For most, it's getting the utilities connected, moving the furniture in, perhaps meeting the neighbours. For me, until I find something a little more permanent, I have to find somewhere to sleep that night. This, depending on my current form of accommodation, could be a lay-by, field or car park. I then need to choose where to position my Big Issue pitch. The pitch must of course be visible, but at the same time, I don't want to get in anybody's way. The pitch needs to be from my perspective, in a position where it doesn't obstruct or upset local traders.

Now, all Big Issue sellers have their own unique way of working. I fit in to what you might call the passive school of selling. I never shout out or ask passers by if they want the magazine. Asking a question invites a response. That response can often be abusive. I really don't need to put myself through that. And besides, I don't want to invade people's space. So I use the only other resources available, my props, two straight shoulders, and a smile. The next task is to distance myself from other street workers; Pollsters, energy switchers, leaflet distributors and Chuggers (charity muggers). These groups of people, I've found, often think they're intellectually and socially far more advanced than the likes of others trying to eke a living on the streets. They feel their jobs are more worthy, have more credence. In fact, they don't actually belong on the streets. They are basically office workers who've been let out for the afternoon. They show little in the way of street etiquette or savvy and make a dismal day a dreary one.

For me, (although there are a few exceptions), at least one of the following criteria are needed to make a good street worker: you add a large dollop of colour to what is now often a drab high street, you don't hassle anyone as they go about their business, and what you see is what you get. To contradict myself, I knew a hassler in Weymouth who I thought was a star. He would go to the stationers every morning and buy a gross of pencils, his stock for the day. He would then walk up and down the High Street, handing people two pencils. Instinctively people would accept them. "Give what you want," he'd say. Invariably a wry smile and a pound coin would head in his direction. An ex-Sergeant in the army, he was also a gentleman. Whether you bought a couple of pencils or whether you told him to get lost, he would always respond with a doff of his cap, a kindly 'good day' and the warmest of smiles. And although a hassler, he was a hassler with morals. He would only buy the expensive pencils in the store because 'the cheap ones are crap, the lead snaps as soon as you sharpen 'em'. Yes, due to mitigating circumstances, the pencil pusher fits neatly into the category that makes my day that little bit brighter.

So, to the chirpy beggar from Devon who will recite you a poem, tell you a joke and do ten one-armed press-ups, all for just a pound... Make 'em laugh! To the wonderful old character in a Bristol underpass who sits all day on a wall with his guitar propped next to him, whilst its case collects the takings from people who assume he's taking a break, when in fact he can't play a note... Hope you get a break soon! To the brilliant, popular portrait artist who lived on the streets and used to trade in Newton Abbot scouring the bins each morning for cardboard to use as canvas, giving away as many portraits as he sold... Keep on drawing the crowds! To Marble Arch Mickey who used to ply his trade outside Marble Arch (of course) one sign displaying 'COLLECTING FOR THE JEWISH BLIND ASSOCIATION' with another below it stating 'THEY WON'T SEE A PENNY OF IT'... Mmmm. To all the brilliantly talented buskers, to all the characters I've met, adding a vibrant hue to a predictable street... Thank you. Keep painting the town red guys!

The final task I need to undertake from my pitch is to distance myself from the local street drinkers. Selling The Issue in Somerset some time ago, I was living in my van on the outskirts of town. Each afternoon after work I would visit the High Street supermarket to get my supplies, and each afternoon I would have to run the gauntlet of five or six street drinkers in the shop doorway. My visiting the store often involved being coerced into giving over a handful of change. A sort of entrance fee.

On one occasion, I stood my ground and refused to hand over my hard-earned cash. And besides, I wasn't doing these guys any favours. The response was threatening, threatening enough to make me seriously consider moving on to another town or, at the very least, shop at another store. You see, these guys assumed we had something in common. And indeed, I'm sure they'd be right. Damaged lives on a journey of healing. A journey that, for some, will be slow and tortuous. One that, for some, will end in failure. Yes, for too many a long day I stood on the road where they now stand. But that road for me is a distant past. My life's walk now takes place on the sunny side of the street. A place that, unfortunately these guys have not yet reached. A place perhaps, they don't yet know exists.

The following day, intending to by-pass the store, I was relieved to find the doorway clear. I entered the shop, picked my supplies and went to the checkout. The young girl duly scanned my goods. When she reached the bottle of wine I intended to purchase, she stated, "Sorry, I can't serve alcohol." "What do you mean?" I asked. Then it dawned on me. "Oh I see, you're not yet 18 so you have to call someone over." The young girl who hadn't yet reached the age of subtlety, then proclaimed in a bellowing, customer announcement type voice, "No, I'm not allowed to serve alcohol to street drinkers." "But... me? Um... street drinker?" I mumbled. She replied with a stony blank stare. I turned to the queue that had now built up behind, to see 12 tutting eyes looking me up and down with open disgust. Humiliated, I abandoned my shopping and scurried out the door.

That evening, talking on the phone to an old friend and customer, I made mention of my shopping experience. My friend was very angry and insisted she telephone the shop manager. The following day she phoned me to say that she'd spoken with him and told him about me and indeed Big Issue vendors in general and that the store's behaviour was not only an insult but potentially harmful to what I and many other vendors had achieved. The manager, in return, asked my friend to pass on his apologies. My friend insisted that he should apologise in person. So I was to expect a visit!

Within minutes, my apology approached me in the form of a young suited man sporting a slightly reddened head. He strode up to me. "Mr Walker?" "Yes," I replied, shaking his hand in a way that hopefully made him feel more at ease. He offered his apologies stating that he'd instructed all his staff not to serve street drinkers and, to the young girl, I, as a Big Issue vendor in slightly less than informal attire, seemed to fit the perceived criteria. As a gesture he handed me a £10 shopping voucher and said I was welcome in his store anytime

That very afternoon, armed with a confident swagger, a still empty shop doorway and a crisp shopping voucher, I once again entered the shop to get my supplies. Once in the store, two things became immediately apparent. One, the same young girl was on the checkout, the other, an absurdly delicate cabernet sauvignon was on special offer at three bottles for a tenner!

Yes, it's always a bit daunting starting in a new town, but once my tasks have been completed, once my first Issue is sold, once my first insult has been graciously received, I'm fine. Let the experience commence.

Once settled in a new town I usually introduce myself to the local postie, informing them that I'll be getting mail and to ascertain what my new postcode is. I often receive letters from friends or postcards from customers on holiday. Not having a recognised residence, I use my pitch as a postal address, i.e. Big Issue Man, Outside Superdrug, Totnes TQ9 5PD.

The occasional postie has a bit of an attitude and refuses point blank to co-operate, instead, preferring to walk past me and post it into the nearest shop. In general, most oblige.

In one particular town, a small town, I was informed by a customer that the postman was a 'grumpy old sod'. A few encounters with him seemed to confirm that. He hated almost everything and everybody. He hated his job, his customers, the government, the opposition, the weather (whatever it was). He hated getting up in the morning, the TV at night and he especially hated the solicitor's office situated next to my pitch. The solicitor's office, closed on Saturdays, was unfortunately armed with a small, very heavily sprung, 'chop yer fingers off' letterbox. A letterbox that wasn't designed to accept the bundles of large mail that Postie was assigned to deliver. He would screw the mail up and ram the shredded mess through the slot. "Only pleasure I get," he remarked.

Postie was not a happy man. It was quite surprising therefore, that when I eventually gathered enough strength to ask him for my postcode, Postie gave a positive response. I think he was a bit of an anarchist and any act that was against the rigid grain of the system, anything that broke his normal routine (delivering mail to a person rather than a building) was fine by him.

A few days later I spotted Postie walking down the street towards me.

His face was positively beaming and his normal funereal walk seemed to have a slight skip to it. What had happened? What had gone wrong? Had he lost the plot and set fire to his mailbag? Had he assassinated the sorting office manager? No, he had his first letter for me.

Over the weeks ahead, any mail for me was always signalled by Postie's huge smile appearing around the corner. Seeing how it made his day, inspired me to go further. I acquired a brass letterbox. As Postie approached, I would hold up my letterbox and he would oblige. I then found a dog glove puppet (actually a fox, but close enough) and would snap at Postie's fingers as he delivered my mail. I now felt responsible for his happiness. If I hadn't received any letters for a while and Postie was on a bit of a downer, I would post a couple of letters to myself, knowing that the following morning his beaming smile would return. Yes, for a while, everyone was happy. I was getting my mail and Postie's days were now often an enjoyable, less fraught experience. Then, once again, it was time for me to leave.

I often think of Postie. That bumbling, lovely, grumpy old sod. Whingeing about the weather, as he screws up the solicitor's mail and rams the shredded mess firmly through their small, heavily sprung, 'chop yer fingers off' letterbox.

When moving to a new town, the one thing I'm absolutely certain of, the one thing that makes that transition so much easier, is that all of the characters I meet in one town will be waiting for me in the next. Whether it be Postie, the bubbly old lady who insists on giving me a slobbery kiss every time she passes, the guy who always insists on telling me a dirty joke, the vicar who brings me a coffee every morning, or the numerous other characters I meet when I enter a new town. I know those exact same characters will eventually emerge (albeit in different guises), I'll meet each and every one of them again.

Postie, like many characters I've met on the streets, provides that dollop of colour. Eccentrics who perhaps provide a topic of conversation, perhaps derision. Characters who evoke a smile, even a glare, are, to me, an essential antidote to an increasingly sterile world.

An elderly couple, with their young grandson, were stood next to my pitch. A young girl ambled past, displaying a luxuriant head of green hair.

"Good God, look at the state of her," the grandmother exclaimed. "If she were a daughter of mine, I wouldn't let her out of the house looking like that." To which the boy remarked: "But Nan, you've got sort of… bluish hair." Nan, slightly taken aback, explained: "No Matthew, this is what's known as a blue rinse." Matthew, not satisfied with the explanation, continued: "Yes, but Nan…" Nan, now wishing she'd never mentioned the girl's hair, interrupted. "Look Matthew," her voice rising an octave, "I've been having blue rinses for years, it's done properly in a salon. Nodding in the girl's direction she said, "I don't stick my head in a bucket of food dye before leaving home."

Matthew, armed only with the unblemished logic of youth bravely responded. "Well, I can't see the difference really Nan." Nan, in defeated tone, turned to her husband and asked sternly, "Did you put the receipt in the bag?" Matthew glanced across and saw me looking, our eyebrows lifting in unison.

One character I met during my first spell of homelessness was Bill, a man of the road, a tramp. Whilst he didn't and never would fit into mainstream society, he was happy. He spent almost his entire adult life roaming around the town centre. Many would stop to chat, some would buy him a meal or a cup of tea, everybody knew him. He was a pivotal element of the community. A focal point. A character. After his death, there was a definite void.

Now I don't pretend to understand why one elderly lady shops every single day, sporting a bouffant that defies the law of gravity, whilst wearing the annual output of Max Factor. I don't know why the man who used to sit next to me on the town bench, needs to say "good morning" to every single passer-by (153 in 30 minutes). They're eccentric, colourful, different and, I believe, an essential element to any community. There's not enough room for us all to be stood bang in the centre of the perceived normality spectrum – we need diversity, we need people perched firmly at the extremes. Communities need eccentrics, communities need colour, communities need "different".

Something that some people, point blank, refuse to accept.

Although not a common occurrence, I do experience the occasional threat or insult. I have to always remain vigilant, looking around for possible problems. I always do my utmost to deflect any possible danger. If someone is walking towards my pitch who appears to me to be a potential threat, I always busy myself, asking a passer by for the time or making sure I'm looking the other way as the perceived threat approaches. Eye contact to be avoided at all costs.

When selling in Tavistock, a man strode purposefully towards me in such a manner that conveyed, this was definitely not my next customer. He walked up to me and with his nose almost touching mine, stated "a piece of shit like you should be hosed off the streets." Then as quickly, strode off again. In Bournemouth, I'd just set up pitch, my sign stated 'Sales assistant required, MUSTN'T be of smart appearance'. A woman approached. With a head looking as though it was about to explode, she yelled, "there's nothing wrong with being smart, I'll have you know". Not grasping what she was talking about, she pointed to my sign. "Aah yes," I responded. "It's an irony madam. A sort of… joke". "Yes," she replied, "a joke on decent, hard-working people".

Over the years, whilst I still don't really understand why people take time and energy out of their world purely to make someone else's world that little more tedious or miserable, I now just put it down to, 'they're having a bad day'. To my surprise, I can honestly say that I've become totally immune to these kinds of insults. The ones that still, and always will, sadden me though, are those involving children. The ones where the disability of bigotry and ignorance are visibly handed down to the next generation. Child abuse at its most subtle.

A couple were approaching my pitch with their six- or seven-year-old daughter walking slightly ahead. As the young girl passed, she held her nose, immediately turning to her parents for approval. They duly obliged. They burst out laughing. When I was selling in Truro, a man and his son walked past. "What's that man doing Dad?" enquired the young boy. His father replied, "very little son, very little."

Yes, there is the occasional cloud…

TRURO

I'm sat here in Truro, by the beautiful cathedral.
My Issues laid out on the ground.
There's a steady flow of tourists with pre-loaded cameras,
And I'm hoping they'll part with a pound.

I watch them adjusting their lenses,
Frustrated they can't find the spot;
Cos the Big Issue man is sat right in the middle
And he's totally ruining the shot.

But wasn't Jesus himself born homeless,
And didn't he roam the streets all his years?
An early day tramp who, for what he believed,
Was abused, scorned, then killed by his peers.

Look I have no meaningful message,
I have no empowering belief;
So please don't besmirch as I sit by the church,
Please don't cause me any grief.

You see, I'm simply sat here selling Issues,
Cos never would I beg, steal nor borrow.
I'm just sat here today trying to make the day pay,
So for me there might be a tomorrow.

I'm sat here in Truro, by the beautiful cathedral
My Issues laid out on the ground.
There's a steady flow of tourists with pre-loaded cameras,
And I'm hoping they'll part with a pound.

…and although very rarely, sometimes, through frustration, I am a little bit naughty.

A woman bought an Issue from me and asked if I smoked. "I do," I confessed. The lady then pulled out a pack of 200 cigarettes. "I wonder if you'd like these," she said. "My sister brought them back from Spain, and I don't really like them." "Thanks very much," I replied, gratefully accepting her gift.

Some 20 minutes later, another woman walked up and asked if I smoked. "I do," I proclaimed. "Oh," she replied, "I don't buy the Issue from anyone who smokes or has a dog." And she walked off.

A while later I saw the woman walking towards me with an Issue in her hand. "Oh, you managed to find a non-smoking, dog-less vendor then?" "Yes," she replied. "I bought it off the vendor outside Body Shop. A lovely young man." "Oh, that'll be my mate Pete," I said. "Yes, he is a lovely young man and yes, he doesn't own a dog, or even smoke. Which, he won't mind me telling you, is quite unusual for a heroin addict."

Yes, through frustration, a little bit naughty…

A customer approached me some time ago and having read some of

the inserts I put into my Big Issues, asked if I could write a poem for his wife. With Valentine's Day looming, he'd organised a romantic evening meal and thought that presenting her with a personalised poem would truly enhance the occasion. And, as her name was Rose, could I write a poem about… a rose!

Now whilst I fully appreciate the overwhelming beauty and miracle of nature, valid concerns over such things as survival were currently crowding my 'let's get emotive' list.

After a long, 'frustrating', non-productive hour…

THOUGHTS OF A ROSE

Why does my poetry need always to rhyme?
Does it make it less valid?
A poetic crime?
Translating my thoughts of a flower into prose,
Scouring my mind for words rhyming with 'rose';
And the flowers' constituents, planning ahead,
Searching for rhyme in a rhyme-barren head.
Now stem… ah! Gem, hem, phlegm;

Smell... bell, fell, dell, it's going well!
(I've tried other ways, using any old word,
But if there ain't no rhyme, it just sounds absurd).
Now hew... dew, blue, new, view.
Petals. Petals?!!... oh sod it, I know what I'll do:
Scrap this rose poem, and start one anew.
I know a young man with a three-legged donkey,
It kept falling over, so he nicknamed it Wonkey;
He had two large dogs, each with bright dewy nose,
one he called Petal and the other one...Rose!

I duly presented my customer with the poem and wished him luck for a successful evening... I haven't seen him since. I do hope he's alright!

But sometimes, inspiration was delivered by the bucket load....

One of my customers, Margaret, approached me and told me her mother had just died. I offered my condolences, and then Margaret told me that prior to her death, her mother had requested that all her belongings be given to The Big Issue.

I immediately thought what a wonderful gesture. It's always thrilled me when the older generation, especially, are so free-thinking in their acceptance of people whom some would perceive as being in a position that was self inflicted or avoidable.

The following week, The Big Issue manager and I arranged to pick up Helen's belongings. Walking through her home, it was obvious that everything was still intact; it remained as it was when Helen 'left'. The only thing missing was Helen herself.

A POEM FOR HELEN

Thank you missus, thank you. I never met you though,
I'm sure you were a super girl, that's the only thing I know.

I don't know what your life was like; I can only take a guess,
I'd say you were quite special, yeah special, nothing less.

Today I saw your living past, trinkets of your life,
Showing different stages; child, woman, wife.

I saw the pictures still in wraps, no time to view the scene.
I felt the air of what has passed and what just might have been.

I saw your treasured household stuff, brass objects, fluffy toys.
I felt the living, breathing home, the laughter, joy and noise.

Then like a child's jack-in-the-box, your life was packed away,
To spring again and give new joy. A legacy, I'd say.

When I next saw Margaret on my pitch, I stressed how wonderful the gesture that her mother had made was, and indeed, the difference it would make to a number of vendors setting up home. I presented her with my poem and after she'd read it, we were both quite overcome.

The scene on my pitch in Plymouth city centre of a stout, well-dressed woman locked in a loving embrace with the Big Issue man, both with tears flowing down their cheeks, is one moment among many I've had that, ironically, I feel so proud of. So fortunate for having had the opportunity to sell The Big Issue, the opportunity to meet so many wonderful people and have so many memorable experiences.

Chapter 3
Religion

As I'm sure most other vendors will testify, Christianity enters our lives on a fairly regular basis. Well, Christianity on the surface, but often anything but.

One religious experience was when I was going through the short, but painful journey from desperately homeless to homeless. I had entered one of my bleakest periods ever. One of those bleak periods that at the time, seem without end. A street advice worker suggested I seek counselling and handed me a leaflet. 'In crisis, in despair? Call Crossways.' I did as the leaflet suggested and arranged an appointment the following day.

It was only when I found that my appointment was to take place on the upper floor of a church that the 2+2 = 4 equation kicked in. Crossways, Church. This is a religious organisation. No matter. As long as there was someone that could help, someone that would listen.

I was ushered into a classroom-sized room where in the corner, by the window, were two chairs facing each other. In one sat a spindly lady in her 50s who invited me to take a seat. I duly obliged. She initially said nothing, merely smiling at me for an uncomfortable minute then suddenly announced," right, tell me what your problem is", almost as if she expected a one line response. I started my story, revealing the route my life had taken to where I was now, here, desperate. As I was speaking, head down, I glanced up to find my counsellor staring out of the window at the traffic! Now even more uncomfortable, I reeled off the remaining events of my life as I would a shopping list, whilst she continued staring out of the window, occasionally rewarding me with a sympathetic nod.

When I'd finished, she gave me a treacly smile and said, "trust me, the only solution to your problems is to accept God into your life". WHAT!! With that, her eyelids slowly closed, her head went back and she entered what I can only describe as a sermonic trance. She just prayed and prayed, and then prayed. I'm sure for her, flinging myself off the nearest bridge was not the problem. The problem was that I met Jesus before I jumped. I walked slowly across the room, the lady oblivious to my leaving. Hey, it was after all, her gig! I opened the door, taking one last glance at my 'praying Christian' and thought, but hey, this is, after all, meant to be my gig. I slammed the door behind me.

Initially I was mortified. The following morning however, with my head obviously having worked the night shift, I awoke and thought the whole thing so surreal, so *Monty Python*-esque, so ludicrous, it brought with it a good yarn, a day of fitful giggles and ultimately the end of my bleak period… Mmm!

Religion makes regular appearances on my Big Issue pitch too. On a daily basis I am approached by people of various religious persuasions. Evangelists, I'm sure, often see me as lost, sinful. They make the assumption that I'm not a Christian and also that I am perhaps living a life that is in turmoil. They, I'm sure, see me as a double glazing salesman does when he happens across a house with all the windows broken. When, in truth, my very standing there selling The Big Issue is testament enough that I am well into the long process of self-building what once was a shattered life.

A man approached me and pointing at my Issues stated: "I don't want one of those things, but I have something you need!" He then pulled out a copy of the New Testament. "Aah," I responded. "I don't actually need one of those."

"Everyone needs one of these," he argued.

"I don't," I stated.

"Look," he said. "I've been handing these out for more than ten years. There is no reason on earth why you don't need this book."

"But I really don't," I answered humbly.

"Why not"? he asked, in a frustrated tone.

"Cos I've got fifteen of 'em already."

On another day, a day I was feeling decidedly chipper, a lady walks up to me, but doesn't buy an Issue or even speak. She just stands adjacent to my pitch and smiles at me. Feeling slightly unnerved, I say, "gorgeous morning".

"Yes it is, but how are you?" she asks in a slow pitiful drone.

"I'm fine," I reply. "I'm feeling wonderful thanks". I suspect this was not quite what she wanted to hear. "I'd like you to read this," she said, as she handed me a leaflet and strode off. The leaflet? A Jehovah's Witness publication about finding happiness. Some time later, she returned. "Have you read the leaflet I gave you?" "I'm sorry love," I replied. "I haven't had chance, been working all day".

"Oh I see," she said, fumbling with a handful of leaflets. "By the way, did I give you the one about death?"

Some religious characters though, even if you don't want it, give absolutely nothing. Selling in Yeovil, Somerset on one occasion, two young American men, Mormons, were evangelising on the street, relaying their message to reluctant passers-by. They stood either side of my pitch making me almost invisible to potential customers. I approached one of them and asked: "As a Christian, how would you feel if by standing there affecting my sales, you could be denying me food and shelter".

His reply? "I'd feel ya aughta get another job."

THE BIG
ISSUE

FREE PAIR OF
STAPLES WITH
EVERY ISSUE

A break for

Ruby-cheeked children sleighing down snow-caked landscape. Santa Claus. Turkey and trimmings. Families sharing gifts around yule log fires. Mistletoe kisses. Lantern lit carollers. Cold hands eased with glasses of hot mulled wine. It's the stuff dreams are made of. Yes, it's that time of year again.

The time when families share a whole day together. Perhaps an early morning walk. The time when grandparents visit, kidnapping the TV remote, while dad plays horseback with the children. When many elderly and lonely feel even more so, laden with memories they'd love the chance to share. When the vicar oversees the annual ritual of a full congregation. Yes, it's Christmas.

When we shop till we drop, ticking off the list of gifts that will no doubt provide as much disappointment as pleasure. When we ask, "what do I buy a ten year old who has everything?" When the stores are never open long enough for last-minute shopping. Christmas, when consumerism

christmas

grabs us by the ankles, spins us upside down and shakes out every last shiny penny. When the absolute joy a parent receives in watching tiny hands peeling away at large presents is matched only by the despair of a parent who can offer little or nothing. Christmas, a time to remember, a time to forget.

Christmas, when wars briefly cease. When handshakes become hugs and we wish good morning to strangers. When spirits are lifted. When year-long family feuds are resolved. When year-long family feuds begin. When fond yet painful memories of those who are no longer here bubble vigorously to the surface. When emotions sit clumsily on the sleeve.

Christmas, a muddled maelstrom of emotion, need, stress, wonderment, frenzy.

Christmas, when the fragrant tone of a children's choir brings with it the calm and innocence of times long gone.

Chapter 4
Moving in

T he ultimate goal for anyone living on the streets, homeless, must surely be permanent accommodation. This, after a few years, was what I set out to achieve. I felt ready for it.

Over the course of six months, I saved every penny to achieve that goal. Then it was happening! I found a wonderful flat in a converted farmhouse. Paying the £600 moving-in costs left me with £300 to keep me going until I'd found some alternative work.

The first night in my new flat was the only time I slept in the bed. The following day I set my dome tent up in the front room. It seemed that this transition was by no means going to be easy. Two weeks later it felt nigh on impossible. I wasn't functioning. I was slowly losing grip of the very qualities I'd acquired over the last years. Fulfilment, happiness, my sense of belonging. Living in the flat was like being plunged into a darkened cellar. Three weeks after moving in, I left. I woke one morning, jumped into my old banger and drove the 60 miles to my next 'pitch'.

This cycle of saving money, moving in, then as quickly moving out again, lasted three years. Each time feeling drained by the ordeal. Each time, feeling guilty of all the effort going to waste. Then it struck me. I'd already got everything I needed. Permanent accommodation was, for me, moving into a flat, but moving out of my home. Something the flat was never going to be. My ultimate aims had already been realised. I was content, at ease with myself, I was in control. This life afforded me the ability to cope. Something I could never do in my other world.

It was a very liberating experience to realise, and then accept, that I didn't need to go through this annual struggle. For now, this was where I wanted to be. For now, this was where I needed to be.

My accommodation over the past years has proved to be as weird, wonderful, wacky and indeed varied as the people I've met and the experiences I've had. From benches to baths, hedgerows to hostels. Tents to train stations. Some forms of accommodation though, did present problems. There were often bedfellows of a slightly unwelcome nature…

After years on the streets, it dawned on me that after long and, at times, tortuous attempts, I'm absolutely useless at being homeless. This, as I'm sure you can imagine, creates for me a bit of a dilemma. Like a fish that can't swim, a surgeon that can't stand the sight of blood, a politician who keeps telling the truth! I, homeless, have not one molecule of survival technique in my body.

My 'colleagues', most of whom I have the greatest respect for, seem to have a unique instinct for survival, a confidence that everything's going to be OK, that something will turn up. And it generally does! No, for them, it just sort of… happens, and for me, it just sort of… doesn't!

One pathetic attempt at survival was when I was offered the use of a tent in the garden of one my customers. The first night in my new home, I forgot to seal the entry flap, waking up to find myself covered head to toe with slugs. Now personally, I've nothing against these creatures – live and let live, that's my attitude. But, as far as I'm concerned, God, when creating the world, must have been on a real downer when he came up with the slug. Anyway, next night, with my tent protected by a wall of slug pellets, I once again, tentatively, attempted sleep, only to wake at 4am finding myself and the contents of my tent floating in water. Apparently during the night I'd kicked open the Velcro strips securing the entrance, rain had come in and due to the tent's poor positioning on the sloping ground, the tent had just… FILLED UP!

Right then! Slug problem sorted, now to cure the flooding. All I need to do is turn the tent around so the slope is towards the door. I think perhaps I've cracked it! I lie down, and with the anticipation of an uninterrupted night, sleep comes quickly. I wake up in the early hours, to find myself and my sleeping bag, absolutely drenched. Opening my eyes, I find that due to the sloping ground, my bag and I have, during the night, slid clean right out of the tent, ending up nestled in a flower bed, yet again covered completely with those slimy molluscs from hell!

Have you ever seen a slug snigger? Trust me, it's not a pretty sight!

My customer, witnessing my pathetic attempts at camping, then offered me use of the outhouse situated at the foot of the garden. The floor, slightly damp, was carpeted with tarpaulin. It was furnished with a folding bed, lamp, a small camping stove and an indoor plant. Well actually, it was an outdoor one really, but one of its branches had clambered through the broken window to form a lush, leafy display at the end of my bed.

My hostess, my customer, would often invite me into 'the big house' for a meal or an evening's TV and, whilst grateful for the gesture, I rarely accepted. On the occasions I did, although attempts were made to put me at ease, I never was. I always felt slightly intrusive, uncomfortable. Besides, after a day on my Big Issue pitch, interacting with friends and customers, I quite enjoyed my own space. The space to mull over the events of today, and the plans for tomorrow.

Then one day, after recently organising and subsequently completing a successful fundraising drive on my pitch, I was rewarded with a weekend away with one of my customers. And what a weekend! (Don't even think it. Platonic I say! Totally platonic!)

My friend met me at the railway station on a Friday morning. We boarded a train, where a first-class carriage transported us to South Cornwall, a taxi then whisked us to our accommodation. A luxury hotel! After booking in, I was shown to my room. I tried to appear nonchalant as I was ushered in (I was anything but successful). The room made a set from *Dallas* look decidedly dingy; four-poster bed, black marble en-suite bathroom, panoramic views across a glistening bay and a bottle of champagne coolly nestled in a silver bucket of ice. Yes, from go to gone, one champagne-fuelled weekend of indulgence. But it wasn't over yet. Not by any means.

Arriving back on the Sunday, I'd been invited to church by some customers. Customers, as unassuming as they were wealthy. I made my own way to the village church and they were there to greet me. After the service, I was driven back to their 'pad' in a 1928 open-top Bentley, unable to resist reeling off royal waves to the local villagers as we passed. They supplied myself and other guests with a cracking lunch, after which, I was finally driven back to my outhouse. And then, it really was over.

On opening my shed door, I scanned the view that welcomed me. Mmm, must prune that damn plant, it's starting to take over. I brewed some tea, and slumped exhausted on my bed. Just me, a warming cuppa and the thoughts of an eventful weekend. It was good to be home.

Sometimes though, accommodation was not only damp and dingy, but also acutely embarrassing. Once, hitchhiking my way back to Exeter, I got stuck in Bristol. It was 2am. Looking for somewhere to sleep, I wandered around, fortunately stumbling across a large green bin with a swivel lid. Lighting a match, I happily discovered its contents contained some cardboard and bubble wrap. Enlisting my 'Blue Peter' mentality, I clambered into the bin and from the contents inside, made blankets and pillow, which were surprisingly comfortable. This, combined with a long

day behind me, made sleep arrive instantly.

Around 8am, I was slowly roused by a low rumbling vibration. For a second or two, I just lay there, listening. Then it hit me. Crumbs! I was on the move! My God! I'm gonna be compacted! I've gotta get out of here. No sooner had these thoughts stabbed my now alert mind than the rumbling stopped. I'd been parked. Phew! Then, looking through a crack in my bin, I was horrified to discover that my home was now situated in a busy shopping precinct, opposite a bus stop full of commuters.

With the threat of a landfill site burial now over, escape without detection was my sole purpose in life. I patiently awaited a lull in the pedestrian traffic, only for it to get busier and busier.

Only one option. GO FOR IT! Sliding open my swivel roof, it selfishly (and with an apparent air of contempt) let out an ear-piercing creak as my head popped up to be met by the gaze of what appeared to be the entire population of Bristol, staring open-mouthed at the apparition slowly rising from the bin. Having got this far however, my initial paranoia soon evaporated, so I coolly climbed out of my makeshift home, brushed myself down and with a confident nod to my captivated audience, wished them a very good day. Without looking back, I walked off to continue my journey to Exeter.

A year or so later, I acquired a car, kindly donated by a customer. Taking out the back seats gave me a compact but comfortable bedroom. I'd found a nice secluded lay-by on the edge of Weymouth and had been there for three weeks with no problem. One evening, just as I'd bedded down for the night, a car pulled up directly in front of me, headlights on full beam. I peered over the top of my bedding and two young guys appeared. Obviously not imagining there would be anyone in the car, they proceeded to break open the driver's door. Covered in a white duvet, I leapt up, arms flailing and let out a huge roar. They screamed, dropped their tools and left that lay-by a damned sight quicker than they'd arrived. Imminent threat over but my cover had been blown. Time to vacate.

I was told Wimborne Minster, a small and apparently friendly town some 20 miles away, was free. I drove up and had a look around. It seemed fine and after a couple of hours searching, I found a suitable lay-by to live in.

Picking my Issues up from the Bournemouth office the following day, I was quite looking forward to my first stint in Wimborne. Steve, another vendor, approached me. "You looking for a van?" "I am, actually," I replied.

With winter just around the corner, I could put some kind of heating in and it would mean I would be less visible to passers-by. Steve informed me that he knew of an old prisoner transport vehicle that a customer of his a farmer, was selling. That afternoon, I went to look at the van. It was ideal. It had a heater, internal lighting and tons of space. I paid for it immediately and arranged to pick it up the following day.

I arrived to collect my van early the next morning. The farmer handed me the keys and as I started the engine, it responded with a bang, a roar, and was then completely engulfed in smoke. I quickly turned off the engine thinking it was on fire. As the farmer slowly reappeared through the clearing haze, he remarked, "smokes a bit mind, might need some work on that engine!" I restarted the van and gave it a few revs, hoping the situation would improve. It didn't. Well, no choice, I've got to get my home to the lay-by. It was Saturday morning, still early, and with 20 miles to go, I decided to set off straightaway before the roads got busy. As I drove out of the farmyard, I looked in the rear view mirror, a pointless exercise. Then as I got out onto the main road, as if by a miracle, a mist descended. A mist like no other, a mist that reduced the traffic to a snails' pace. A mist that easily disguised the fact that my exhaust was churning out more noxious smoke than a Bob Marley concert.

For 18 miles I, along with other drivers, crawled along. All, except me, oblivious to the fact that the 'mist' behind was far denser than the mist ahead. Then, with less than two miles to go, the mist disappeared as quickly as it had arrived. Cars approached me with lights flashing, horns blowing. I responded with a smile and a cheery wave. The last two miles seemed like forever. I stuck my foot down, continued smiling and waving and then I was there. My lay-by, my new home.

Over the next couple of weeks, Wimborne, in general, took kindly to me. I looked forward to staying there for a few months. Then one particular evening, after walking back home, I noticed an awful stench in my lay-by. On further investigation I found, on the bank, a full head of women's hair. Oh my God! Looking further, I discovered that next to it was a bag of rotting flesh. Oh my God! I nudged the bag with my foot and could see it contained intestines and 'stuff'. Oh my God!! Right, don't panic. It's nothing to worry about. Panicking, I sprinted back into town to find help, but the police station was closed. I was a bit loath to ring 999 for fear I was overreacting. I needed a second opinion!

I decided to go to the pub, The Oddfellows, where I sometimes stopped for a pint after work. As I walked in, the barmaid greeted me. I approached the bar and, head down, whispered my dilemma and asked if she knew someone who might accompany me back to my lay-by to give me their opinion as to what I should do. The barmaid shouted across the bar "Jim! Steve! Quick! Would you go with Graham? He thinks he may have found a dead body in his lay-by!" Great.

We all got into Jim's car and made our way up to my lay-by. Steve, on seeing the scene, said "Christ, we've gotta 'phone 999." So as Jim and I carried on inspecting and chewing over the contents of the bag, we left Steve to make the call. Within minutes, a police car arrived. The officer, who introduced himself as PC Harris, inspected the scene and immediately called for backup. He took our names and 'addresses' and dismissed Steve and Jim, informing them that they may wish to speak to them again. As they left my lay-by, back-up arrived. The policemen inspected the 'corpse'. "We need scene of crime officers," said one. The others all nodded in agreement. So they called for more backup.

With my lay-by now under siege, sealed off, five patrol vehicles, forensics rushing about in while boiler suits and more flashing lights than downtown Las Vegas, I sat on the bank, head in hands, thinking 'what on earth have I done to deserve this?' PC Harris approached me. "So you're living up here are you?" he asked accusingly. "Yes officer," I replied. "I sell The Big Issue in town." "Well," he responded, "we need to search you and your vehicle." "Why?" I asked, "I'm the one who got you up here." "Well, I'm sorry sir, but the emergency call we had from your friend was, 'woman's body found in lay-by. Big Issue man sleeping rough there'." Great! Thanks Steve. So you not only tell the police that someone's been murdered, but also who's done it! After searching my vehicle and finding nothing, attention turned back to the bag. After much prodding and probing its contents, fortunately for me (unfortunate for the animal) they concluded that it was the partial remains of a cow, and on further investigation, the hair turned out to be a wig. So after three hours, I was once again alone in my lay-by. Well, not quite alone!

The following evening, the stench from the bag was unbearable so I decided to move my van up-wind to the other end of the lay-by. Safely parked up, I was so much looking forward to an uneventful night. Almost immediately I heard the distant but distinctive drone of an emergency vehicle. I listened to it get louder and louder, then flashing lights came into view. Crumbs, it was two fire engines! And they were coming into my lay-

by! What the hell was going on? The fire engines came to a halt, just as a police patrol car pulled up behind me. PC Harris did not look amused.

Apparently, as I had started the engine on my van, the large plume of smoke had been seen by two passing motorists, both of whom dialled 999, reporting a vehicle on fire in the lay-by.

Head in hands time again! I offered my profuse apologies to the officers, and making sure everything was in order, the fire crews drove off. PC Harris, before leaving, wished me goodnight and with a profound smirk, uttered, "see you tomorrow then?" Methinks, time to vacate… again!

Now most of the time I slept alone. On occasion I didn't…

It had been a good day for me. Not only was it my birthday, but the sun had made its first appearance in five days. Excellent! Having already received cards and lovely presents, I was determined, if nothing else, to make my birthday a memorable one.

With the money I'd saved I decided to go for a meal and then watch a film. With my last trip to the cinema being over 12 years ago, it was sure to be memorable.

Sat on the bus awaiting its departure to Plymouth, one of my customers who is also a very supportive friend, boarded the bus and handed me a choc ice and a £5 note. Wow! A lovely end to a special day and soon to be followed by a relaxing evening.

I entered the cinema with half an hour to spare and took my seat. Awaiting the start of the film, I sat and thought about the past week and that, due to the latest bout of bad weather, I still had lots of Issues left. I would have to ensure an early start in the morning to have the slightest chance of selling them all. This problem continued to niggle as the cinema slowly filled. As the film started, I decided not to worry and enjoy the show.

It started well, definitely my sort of film, but with a sound meal inside me, the warmth of the cinema and a long day on The Issue, twenty minutes later, I fell asleep!

Awaking with a jolt some half an hour later, in a deep state of confusion, I stood up and shouted at the top of my voice, "my God, what time is it?!" As I finished shouting, the realisation of where I was and what I'd just done, hit me like a punch in the face. With 200 eyes staring at me, I stupidly remained standing, uttering apologies to one and all. I sat back in my seat, wishing earnestly to be somewhere else, anywhere else. I slunk back, pushing myself deeper and deeper into my seat, desperately wanting, no, needing, to be part of it. The embarrassment soon evaporated though, as ten minutes later… I fell asleep again!

I was next awoken by a queue of people trying to clamber over my sprawling legs. I looked up to see the credits rolling. Quickly grabbing my coat, with head down, I darted towards the exit then out onto the street and freedom! Yes, memorable indeed.

In terms of quality though, my accommodation over the years has incrementally improved. From sleeping rough to tent, followed by outhouse, car, Transit van, and now finally, 12 years later, a rather aged, but nevertheless functional and rather swish motorhome. Yes, both my motorhome and I, have between us, clocked up many memorable miles to arrive at where we now stand.

THE BIG
ISSUE

SALES ASSISTANT
REQUIRED.
MUSTN'T BE
OF SMART
APPEARANCE

Chapter 5
Out to lunch

A s a Big Issue vendor, food has continually been a cause for concern. Not the lack of it. In general, too much. Far too much. And although I've received many offers to visit customers' homes for a meal, bed, bath and on occasion for more 'interactive pursuits', I rarely accept the invitation. After what is often an intense day on my pitch, I do look forward to that bit of space, look forward to, for a while, not being a Big Issue man. On one occasion, though, I did accept.

Selling The Issue in Newton Abbot, I was living in the back of my car in a lay-by, some two miles out of town.

One particular Saturday on my pitch, June, a regular customer, bought The Issue and asked if I'd like to share Sunday lunch with her and her family. I'd got to know June and her husband quite well over the past weeks, they were really laid back and very accepting of my position so I thought it might be a quite relaxing afternoon, with the conversation not focused on homelessness and The Big Issue as on a previous visit to a customers' home. "I'd love to," I replied. They gave me directions to their home, which happened to be just a couple of hundred yards from my lay-by. "Good," said June. "Well, bye for now and we'll see you at 3 o'clock on Sunday."

Now another good friend in Newton Abbot was a local newspaper reporter, Sue. Through her, I'd been featured in the local press on a number of occasions. It seemed I would only have to sneeze and it would be splattered across the front page.

Later that afternoon Sue came up to my pitch. "How long do you plan on staying here today Graham?" she enquired. "I've got quite a few Issues left," I answered. She explained, "someone from Paignton has just rung the newspaper office asking if you were on your pitch. Apparently they read an article about you in the paper and would like to come and have a chat with you." "Well, I'll be here for a couple of hours, Sue. I'll be going about 4 o'clock," I said. "OK," replied Sue. "I'll go and let them know."

An hour later, as I looked down the road, a couple were walking briskly towards me. "This is them," I said to myself. And indeed it was. They introduced themselves as Mary and Richard. "Nice to meet you," I said. I was intrigued. What did they want? And why travel all this way? "Me and Richard read the article about you in the paper and we'd like to know a bit about you, wouldn't we Richard?" Richard nodded in agreement. "And we hope you won't take offence but we'd like to invite you to our home for lunch on Sunday, wouldn't we, Richard?" Richard not having quite finished nodding over the last question nodded more vigorously. "Ah well… um, I'd love to," I replied, "but I'm living just outside of town. I wouldn't be able to make it across to Paignton." "Oh that's no problem, Graham," she beamed. "We could come over and pick you up, couldn't you Richard?" Nod!

Dilemma. They'd travelled a 20 mile round trip to invite me to lunch. How could I be so callous as to refuse? "Well, what time would we be eating?" I enquired. "We have lunch at 12:30 precisely so Richard could pick you up at 12:00 if that's OK." "That'll be fine, just fine," I muttered. "Good," said Mary. Richard nodded. I gave them directions to my lay-by and they walked off waving continually until they were out of sight.

Now I'm not a big eater, I'm more of a snack man myself, so how on earth was I going to cope with two Sunday lunches in the space of two hours?

Richard arrived at exactly midday. "Good morning," he uttered. "Lovely morning." I replied. Nod! The next words Richard spoke were as we arrived at the house. "Here we are then." As we walked into the front room, Richard spoke again. "Why on earth have you moved all the furniture around?" "Well," said Mary, "I thought Graham would be more comfortable sitting over there by the window." I could sense from Mary's face that had I not been in the room there would be a bit of a 'tiff' happening. Hard to imagine from first meeting Mary and Richard, but the atmosphere was quite tense. Once I was seated, for the next half hour Richard beavered away in the kitchen whilst Mary grilled me on how I'd become homeless.

At 12.30 precisely, lunch was ready. Fortunately it was a help yourself affair, I helped myself to minute portions of vegetables and chicken. After all, this meal was, for me, an aperitif. Mary scanned my plate. "You can have as much as you want Graham, there's plenty to go around." Whilst protesting I didn't have much of an appetite, Mary piled mounds of food onto my plate saying, "don't be silly, we all have to eat." So for the next half an hour I ate, but for all my efforts, the mountain of food barely reduced in size. Time was not on my side, so I ate again. As I reached what could be termed base camp, Mary finally suggested, "if you've had enough leave the rest, then perhaps we can take the dog for a walk."

"DOG WALKING?" My mind yelled. "DOG WALKING? I don't think so! It's ten to two. I've got another lunch date in an hour." During the dog walk, Mary told me that she'd met her husband whilst she was in the Salvation Army. He was a client, a reformed alcoholic. When she and her husband were divorced, she felt ostracised from, and then left, the Army. It was then that her and Richard's relationship developed. I found it quite uncomfortable being given such personal information from a complete stranger. It was apparent that Mary was quite lonely. She simply needed someone to talk to.

Dog walk over, we arrived back at the house. It was now twenty past two. I offered my apologies and told Mary I needed to get going as I had a lot of letters to write. "OK," said Mary. "We'll give you a lift back home, but you must stop for a cuppa before you go." "Of course," I beamed. "A cup of tea. Wonderful."

It was twenty to three when Richard nodded to Mary's request to put his coat on. Five minutes later, we were on our way. Come on Dick I thought, fly like the wind, put yer foot down and fly like the wind, but Richard didn't do "putting yer foot down".

We arrived back at the lay-by at five past three. I thanked Mary and Richard for an unforgettable time and they promised to come and visit me on my pitch the following week. As they drove off Mary and I waved continuously until the car was out of sight. I then legged it down the hill to my next lunch.

I rang June's bell and the door opened almost instantly. I offered apologies for my lateness. As June ushered me in, the door opened to the dining room. There were nine or ten people awaiting my arrival, all sitting around a dining table supporting the biggest chicken I'd ever seen. June invited me to take a seat and, in what seemed to be a sinister tone, said, "I do hope you're hungry."

Normally, I wouldn't have to go for food. Food, more often, would come to me, usually in the form of a pasty! Now, whilst I appreciate people's kindness and compassion, the fact is, I hate pasties, however they come. Rough puff, cheese and onion, shortcrust, beef and stilton. Even the traditional Cornish. I hate the taste, the smell, the shape. I can't even stand the sight of the damn things.

Unfortunately, as a Big Issue vendor, this is a major drawback in my working life around Devon and Cornwall's coastline. The pasty year, for me, is made up of two seasons. There's summer (the passive pasty season) when, from early morning till late evening, I lay witness to huge families with huge noses stuck in huge pasty-filled bags being pursued, like a trawler on heat, by huge seagulls mopping up the trail of pasty debris. (Look, I'm sorry if I sound a mite bitter. I have every respect for tourists or indeed anyone that feels the need to walk through the town with their face stuck in a pasty bag. It's just that my hatred of the things is so intense

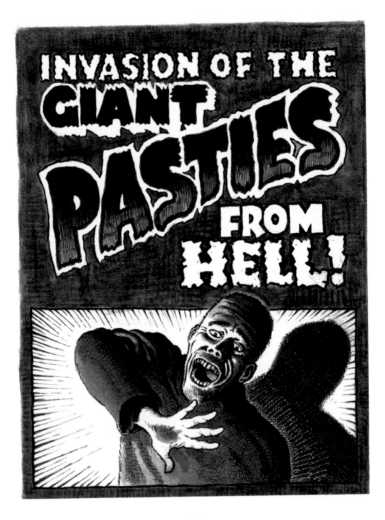

that it completely overwhelms my normally compassionate, caring and accepting nature).

When the tourists arrive, before unpacking, before scolding the kids for turning the car into a mobile tip, even before unbuckling gran from the back seat, off they go, in search of the nearest 24-hour pasty shop. (I'm doing it again, aren't I?) Desperate for their annual fix, as I stand there, eight hours a day, seeing, smelling, breathing pasty.

And then, as autumn heralds a pause in the pasty procession, as the pasty haze diminishes sufficiently to finally allow the fresh sea breeze to penetrate, just as the pasty has found a comfortable little niche at the back of my mind… WINTER HAPPENS! Pasty season two.

Summer over, the tourists long gone, the pasty sales graph takes a seemingly fatal nose-dive. Pasty shop proprietors pace up and down their empty shops, pausing occasionally to stare at the barren streets. Reflecting on those heady, halcyon, pasty-filled summer days. Then, as the temperature gradually falls, with a faint, almost discernible rumble, the pasty machine slowly, very slowly, kicks back into life.

My first ever 'donation' came on a crisp December morning. Stood on my pitch outside Boots in Plymouth, selling my wares, innocently going about my business, a lady walked purposefully towards me, excitedly waving a bag. As she presented it to me, I instinctively held out my hand. Slapping the bag into my palm, she proclaimed, "Here you are love, a nice hot pasty. That should keep you going." Then briskly strode off. Aghast, I just stood there, dazed, arm outstretched, with the 'thing' peering at me through the end of its bag.

With another four pasties arriving on my pitch that day, all accepted with feigned, extreme gratitude and a polite, uncontrollable grimace, I realised I had a problem. Fortunately, my clutch of pasties, by the end of the day, had been redistributed to other street people. But I knew I still had a problem, and that problem was tomorrow. There had to be a solution. After careful consideration, I decided honesty was indeed the best policy.

The following day, my first pasty arrived at the seemingly bizarre and most unexpected time of 9.30am. Slightly taken aback, I soon gathered myself enough to remember the previous evening's well-practiced lines. Huge smile. Shoulders back. Here we go! "Thank you so much for thinking of me, it's a wonderful gesture, but the truth is, I don't actually like pasties."

I knew instantly, and it's something that even now still haunts me and something I should have foreseen. My polite refusal was one glaringly huge mistake. (A mistake I would never make again). As my customer held aloft the now surplus pasty, as she slowly grasped what I'd just said, her round kindly face took on a sort of confused astonishment, then turned to one of hurt and rejection. Mine took on a genuinely pained expression of guilt, thinking, how could I have been so bloody selfish!

*The record number of pasties graciously received in one day: 18! (Dorchester. December 1999)

Some food 'donations' though, weren't quite as gracious...

Selling in a seaside town during the summer, a lady approached me. Obviously struggling to find an adjective that wouldn't offend, she asked, "are there any more of... eh, people like you in town?" What, 5'5", slightly balding and gagging for a cup of tea? I thought. "People like me?" I responded. "Yes," she said. "You know, people who are... eh, destitute and stuff." "Aahh, I see, well, there are a few of us around." "Well the thing is, I own the delicatessen over the back there," she said, pointing over my shoulder. "Now when I close at the end of the week I've often got lots of stuff left, you know, pasties, cakes etc. that won't keep the weekend. It seems such a shame to throw them out, so I thought if you and your... eh, friends were hungry, you could all come across when I close on Saturday and I'd let you have them for half price." Stunned!

Chapter 6
Ripples

Early summer, living in Penzance, I returned home one day to find the extreme weather conditions we were experiencing had all but destroyed my tent and scattered my belongings across a field. I'd been in Penzance more than three months now. Perhaps it was time for a change. I telephoned The Big Issue office in Exeter to enquire what pitches were available. As soon as I heard the word Barnstaple, I was on my way.

I was always anxious to get to Barnstaple. My last visit there was two years earlier, to attend my nephew Darren's funeral. Darren, my sister's son had suffered all his life with Muscular Dystrophy and had, at 21, died at Littlebridge House, the children's hospice there. This would be the first time I would move to a pitch specifically in order to do some fundraising.

A couple of weeks after my arrival, a farmer called Charles allowed me to set up camp on his land. After a high profile six months on my pitch, I was ready. My fundraising stint involved me selling The Issue dressed in 1930s-style top hat and tails (accompanied by the music of Fred Astaire) complete with silk scarf, patent leather shoes etc. I did look the business. For me, it felt good. The Big Issue man, the smartest guy in town.

For my efforts, I asked the local community to sponsor me by buying a Christmas gift for a child. These were to be distributed to the Children's Hospice and Barnstaple Poverty Action Group. The response was phenomenal. Over 3,000 gifts and £1,500 in cash. A truly wonderful experience.

Just after Christmas, prior to departing for pastures new, I was informed that I'd been chosen as Barnstaple's Citizen of the Year. (Keys to the city would have been nice). My prize was an all expenses night in the Royal Fortescue hotel and an evening at the theatre.

My last visit to the theatre had been a few weeks earlier, just after my fundraising had finished. I'd been invited to attend the official reception where Noel Edmonds was booked to switch on the Christmas lights. When I arrived, there was a huge crowd outside. I fought my way through and reached the barrier. Tossing my backpack over, I scaled the barrier, only to be forced back by a security guard. "But I've been invited to the civic

reception," I pleaded. He looked me up and down and then, without saying a word, walked off. I should have worn my top hat and tails I thought. Two attempts later, with credentials eventually checked, I was finally allowed through.

I was led upstairs and invited to help myself to the buffet. Now this wasn't your average post wedding disco buffet. This was a posh job. Not a vol-au-vent in sight. I couldn't even recognise what I was eating! But I ate it anyway. In fact, a lady, (who I think was the mayor's wife) and I devoured the majority of it between us. Washing it down with a couple of glasses (possibly four) of a rather delicate French number, I was interrupted by the organiser. She invited me to meet a few people.

Well, the room was awash with dignitaries. This was Ascot 'indoors'. More air kisses than you could shake a stick at. After being introduced to a few of my fellow guests, I was formally introduced to Mr Edmonds and his family.

Now Noel's career hadn't been going too well of late. This was during his few years stuck in the TV wilderness, so I imagine being invited to switch on Barnstaple's Christmas lights was quite a 'big deal' for him. Shortly after 'formally' meeting Noel, I returned to the food, whilst he was summoned to the balcony to perform the 'switching on' ceremony. As he was making his speech, I, with a mouthful of posh buffet, inched myself up behind him and gave a royal wave to the crowd below.

I could see the look on their faces; what's The Big Issue man doing up there? And who's that bloke with him?

Whilst in Barnstaple, I met a young man who, like me, lived on the streets. Tom was a beggar, armed only with a penny whistle, three tunes and the lifeless complexion of a heroin addict. He was a sweet guy and we'd often stop work for a chat, but he was a guy tormented both physically and mentally by the evil, iron-like grip of heroin. A grip so strong that even the fatal (accidental) overdose of his girlfriend a year earlier couldn't loosen it. A grip that, having taken everything Tom had, was now on target for its ultimate goal – Tom himself!

Tom's 'pitch' was just along the street from mine. His working day generally consisted of two shifts, each varying in length, dependent on how long it took to reach the magic figure that would see him scurrying off to his dealer for his twice-daily fix.

My stay in Barnstaple, as in many other towns, was memorable. I made some wonderful friends and met some fantastic people. After I left, I knew, as in other towns, that it was highly unlikely that I'd ever see anyone from Barnstaple again.

Three years later, whilst visiting friends in Plymouth, a young man strode up to me. "You're Graham!" he announced. "I am," I agreed. He shook my hand firmly. "I'm Tom, Tom from Barnstaple." I was stunned. The two grey hollows that had once passed for eyes were now bright and alive. His once drug-drenched body was now upright and eager. "I'd like to thank you Graham, you did me a huge favour." I was puzzled. I hadn't seen Tom in more than three years. He explained that, after I'd left, there was an abundance of goodwill in the town and with no Big Issue seller there, Tom became its recipient. I think the people of Barnstaple were now equipped with a new perspective of what homelessness and, indeed, homeless people were about, and Tom was now the focal point for that understanding. He talked excitedly about how his 'takings' went up fivefold. "It was great," he said. "All these people walking around with a pound coin and no Issue seller to give it to, so they gave it to me!" And apparently, as lots of people were unaware that I had left, they would approach Tom to ask after me, at the same time feeling obliged to throw a coin into his hat. Tom's rise in earnings was just as importantly matched by the relationships, the friendships he started to form. This, in turn, led to him being offered a flat.

With his increased income and the help from his new friends, his flat very soon became a home. Now, for the first time since his girlfriend died, Tom felt he had something to lose. Tom, although still on heroin, now had a reason to live.

He left Barnstaple some six months later, to get away from the heroin environment he was so closely associated with, to start afresh in Plymouth. Although an immense struggle, the next six months saw him reduce and finally break the bonds of heroin addiction. As Tom was talking, a young girl approached. It was Tom's new girlfriend. They'd just set up home together and Tom was now about to start his second year at Plymouth University.

I felt totally humbled. I was amazed at the transformation Tom had achieved. Whilst in Barnstaple I had, if you like, created a bit of a splash in the town, but unbeknown to me, after I'd left, the ripples continued. Tom had taken full advantage of these and, in turn, embraced its power to support him in achieving what was then the unthinkable. Now, who's to know what positive effects, what splashes Tom himself will now make and, indeed, what effect the ripples he creates may have on others.

My latest fundraising stint, performed on the streets of Weston-super-Mare, as in Barnstaple, also had a strong motive behind it. I was selling the Issue in a small pedestrianised area on the streets of Bridgwater when a man walked up and handed me two pasties and a five pound note. In response to his kindness, I gave him a copy of a booklet I'd had printed. The booklet, a concise version of what you are now reading, also contained my email address. A week later, checking my mail at the local library, this same man, Mark, had left me a message. It informed me that he'd enjoyed my book, was a dentist in Weston-supe-Mare, and was happy to provide whatever dental treatment I needed, 'on the house!' Wow.

Now I'd imagine it must be this thing with dentists. When they meet someone, their eyes inadvertently examine the contents of your mouth. Mmm, Upper right 4. cap. Lower left 6, missing. Upper left 2, filling. At the time my mouth contained no more than thirteen teeth, (eight and a half functional), so whilst grateful for the offer, I was a little concerned Mark had bitten off more then he could chew, so I didn't respond immediately. I was already resigned to the fact that the contents of my mouth were now beyond economical repair. I was reticent too, accepting such a huge gift from a complete stranger. A week later, another email arrived. This time from the dentist's wife. A lovely message where she too said she enjoyed my little book and urged me to take up the offer of treatment.

Now I've lived a life lucky enough to have made many dear friends and had many wonderful experiences. A life fortunate enough to have received many offers of help. Help often arriving at the time perhaps when I needed it most. Offers of help, through pride, independence or whatever, I have generally declined. The offers I have accepted, offers that have always been unconditional, in accepting them, I have in turn, needed to make them anything but. What comes around must, for me, go around. Now the obvious opposite of that condition is the well worn cliché, 'what goes around comes around'. Something I don't necessarily buy into. From experience that doesn't always happen. And why should it. If I do good, I don't expect or even need that good at some stage to return with a cursory slap on the back. No, you do good, you do it unconditionally. You do it not as a favour (sounds a bit reluctant), or for loyalty points, or to gain that extra foothold in the Promised Land. No, you do it to help someone you have the ability to help.

'What comes around' is different It's not something that's earned, not warranted. It's chancing upon good fortune, being the recipient of someone else's unconditional help. For me, that is so different. When you receive that help, that energy, untainted by clauses, if you're in a position to accept it, it's as pure as it is powerful.

Now that energy could finish its journey with you, that's fine. Someone offered help, you accepted it. Recipient and donor both satisfied. You can though, take that help, that energy, use of it what you will, then once invigorated, once strong enough, re-inject the same impetus you've extracted and send that ball of compassion on its merry way to perhaps fortune others.

So I accepted the offer. On condition, I would in turn, raise the £2,000 the surgery would have cost, and donate that money to the Children's Hospice. So my van and I moved to a lay-by in Weston-super-Mare and I set up pitch in between Topshop and Boots, 200 yards from the dental surgery. Let treatment commence.

After four months, with the surgery almost complete. It was time for me to start fundraising. This time though, it was a slightly different experience. I was fundraising in a large town. A town where, unlike before, I hadn't yet been totally accepted, totally trusted. From my perspective, it was a very big ask to invite people to hand over money to me, in the hope that it would reach its final destination. I once again, needn't have worried. The experience did carry with it though, elements that I hadn't experienced in other towns. Elements that turned what should have been an organic, 'what comes around goes around' moment, into one that didn't quite make it.

When I enter a new town, it's quite surprising how much grief I get from local shops and businesses. They either turn on to what I'm doing, or they most definitely don't. In one particular town, I was standing in front of a pillar adjoining two shops. The owner of the shop to my right came out and suggested I move down the street as he reckoned I was 'frightening his trade away'. I explained to him: "Look sir, it's a Ying Yang thing. Embracing your logic, the people walking towards your store from the left might see me, and indeed be frightened away, so consequently the people approaching your store from my right might see me and be frightened in!" He didn't appreciate my philosophy so I took him up on his suggestion.

It was to be no different in Weston. However hard I'd tried to engage with the Boots staff, other than the young security guard who'd come out for a chat during his fag break, not one of them had ever said 'good morning', made any eye contact, or acknowledged me in any way whatsoever. Not, of course, that I deserved, expected, or indeed needed them to. It's just nice to get on. Then one morning, having got my Fred Astaire gear out of storage, I once again donned top hat and tails. The local press were taking a picture to publicise my fundraising that was due to start the following week. The Boots' staff were over me like a rash, a nice rash though. Yes, my relationship with them, from that moment on, changed forever.

The fundraising took a week to complete, far quicker than I'd ever imagined. This was largely due to my new found friends in Boots raising over £1,000 towards my target. Thank you ladies.

Yes what came around was shiny new teeth, a shiny new smile, and just as importantly, shiny new friends. None shinier than Mark, my dentist and his lovely wife Sylvia. And what went around was over £2,800 for the Bristol Children's hospice and two local homeless projects.

The following day at 2.30pm, I handed £800 to the two local homeless projects, whilst a local volunteer came to my pitch to accept the £2,000 donation for the hospice. The lady in question was the ex-mayor of Weston. If I was asked to describe her in two words, they would have to be, overbearing and officious. She introduced herself, and on seeing my sign stating the total raised was £2,800, remarked, "wonderful effort, and I understand that Boots have also raised £1,000." At this point I lost it. You see, as a Big Issue vendor, fundraising for the local community, there are certain people who just can't see past the anomaly of it. So I have not only to be above board and squeaky clean (I couldn't be otherwise), I have to appear to be so as well. But here I was, a babbling wreck, simply trying to hand over £2,000. "Aah well," I mumbled. "No actually um, this total is um... inclusive of... eh, that." Not surprisingly, the answer didn't register. She became even more overbearing, as I felt increasingly vulnerable and nervous. Then, after finally convincing her the total raised was indeed ONLY £2,800, before withdrawing the knife, she gave it a little twist, and said, "Oh, never mind. It's still a good effort. I too support the hospice you know; during my time as mayor, my appeal raised over £24,000." I almost apologised. It was now 3 o'clock. Time to vacate.

THE BIG
ISSUE

PLEASE DO NOT
ASK FOR CREDIT
AS REFUSAL
OFTEN OFFENDS

Chapter 7
Friends

I'm sure most people have witnessed someone scouring rubbish bins. Surviving on others' discarded leftovers. Or seen the guy satisfying his nicotine habit with soggy, heel-trodden dog ends peeled from the pavement. It's likely your head supplies such thoughts as, 'how could anybody reach such a position?' Well there are as many answers to that as there are people living on the streets. But homeless, sleeping rough, one can become Neanderthal. Now to most, it's second nature to wash and brush your teeth before work. Perhaps a post lunch floss, a shower in the evening, the occasional colonic irrigation after an over indulgent supper. But homeless, on the streets, all basic instincts that together constitute health, hygiene, well being, are often lost. The habits of washing, brushing teeth etc., are often preceded by the habit of 'not'.

At the peak of my homeless career, I would go weeks without washing, brushing teeth or changing clothes. Grim? To me and others around me, not so. I, as many others who have spent time on the streets, become feral, untamed. Not washing for a day or two causes discomfort. Not washing for weeks, mixing only with those who have also lost the habit of hygiene, that discomfort evolves into 'why bother', then eventually, 'normal'.

Now it may sound contradictory when I say there were strong murmurings in the camp that Scouse Al had perhaps taken the habit of 'not', just a tad too far. To a level, in fact, never seen before. You see Scouse Al's feet and subsequently his socks had for weeks, been firmly locked, festering inside a cheap pair of trainers. Yes, incredible as it sounds, for over two months, day and night, not once had Scouse Al's trainers left his feet.

Now at this point, I have a vision. Whilst most people shower every day, a bi-product of that shower is the slaughter of innocent bacteria, bacteria that will never experience the pleasure of adolescence, (how could you!). But within the confines of Scouse Al's trainers, evolution was afoot! His bacteria were given the freedom to thrive, to procreate, form little bacterial families. Villages developed, evolving into townships. One smart ass even invented a little wheel! Yes, evolution continued apace. Sky scraper cities. Digital technology. Two cheap trainers housing two festering

feet, two parallel planets of bacterium. But unbeknown to Al, circumstances were looming. An event was soon to occur. An event that would leave Scouse Al powerless. Yes, for the worlds of Bacterium, Armageddon was just one sweaty step away. Al's socks and trainers were about to part company.

It was an intensely hot summer's day, ideal conditions for the worlds of bacterium. Al, his trainers and I had arranged to meet friends on Plymouth Hoe where there was a free, one-day music festival. The festival was in full swing when we arrived. We decided to first visit the local supermarket for provisions. Al, being fairly well-known in the area, walking through the crowd, we were stopped two or three times and handed money to purchase items for other people. Not knowing that at the top of the lighthouse overlooking the Hoe, were two policemen, watching and recording our every move. Before setting off to the store, we decided to relieve ourselves in the toilet block. Stepping out of the toilets, we found ourselves surrounded by a solid ring of policemen. My initial thought that we were caught up in some fancy dress festival conga, proved well off the mark. We were actually being arrested for suspected drug dealing.

We were bustled past the hippy encampment to where the police hung out. There, we were placed in a van housing two cells with a wire mesh partition. Each cell furnished with a seat, a table and a police interrogator. After intense and lengthy questioning, it was surely obvious to all that we were totally innocent of any wrong doing. They could surely see it was a losing battle. They could have pulled out there and then. But no, doggedly they moved on to the next stage of the game. A strip search! I gave Al a furtive glance. Yes mate, the day had finally arrived. For me, no problem. I'd washed my feet only two weeks earlier. They'd even been out for an airing just the day before. But Al! I contemplated turning informer and telling the police about the 'feet' issue, perhaps saving them from an experience that could scar them for life. I said nothing.

I slowly removed my coat, making sure that Al remained well ahead of me in the strip stakes. Halfway into unbuttoning my shirt, the words 'now yer trainers' came from Al's cell. Showtime! I continued fumbling with my buttons as I watched Al slowly undo his laces. I envisioned mayhem in Bacterium. Their apocalypse was fast approaching. Bacterial carnage on a scale never seen before.

Initially it was a bit of an anti-climax. Al just nonchalantly kicked off his trainers, and then… nothing! But then it happened! I can only describe it as the loudest silent explosion I've ever heard. This was followed by an invisible, but deathly, mushroom-cloud stench that bought the van and its occupants to their knees. I thought, crumbs, if you could bottle this stuff, you'd have the ultimate weapon of mass destruction. The next line I'll leave to the policeman who was currently staggering to the door. "What the fuck! Get 'em out! FOR CHRISSAKES. GET EM OUT!"

We were unceremoniously bundled out of the van, rapidly followed by our clothes and, of course, Scouse Al's trainers. I took this as being a unanimous Not Guilty verdict. With Scouse Al's feet being judge and jury. We left our interrogators crouched on the grass positively gasping for breath. I turned to Al. "Come on mate, get those bloody trainers on. Shop closes in ten minutes." Six months later, Scouse Al would become an ex-Big Issue vendor, living in a flat with his partner, and have feet you could eat your dinner off.

Scouse Al was one of a group of very dear friends I'd met during my Plymouth days. A group that all happened to arrive in the same place at the same time. A group that instantly clicked. Those that are still alive, remain the dearest of friends. Those who have, for whatever reason, died sadly reinforce the statistic that the life span of the long-term homeless is 49 years.

One of that group was Adam, a fellow Big Issue vendor. We instantly connected. It was one of those relationships that I'm sure everyone has experienced. A meeting of minds. A relationship, a friendship, that was never a struggle, never awkward. A friendship where the giving and receiving were naturally matched. An unconditional friendship, where nothing was unforgivable, nothing unforgettable. A safe, comfortable friendship. A friendship in sync! Yes, Adam and I had, between us, more than many, wonderful, amazing, painful and unforgettable experiences.

Adam was a good, corkingly good-looking bloke. Good-looking to the point of pretty. But dangerous. Not to anyone else. No, Adam was only a major hazard to himself.

You see, Adam lived life in the fast lane. A lane that, for Adam, was at times frustratingly slow. A fast lane that ultimately ended our relationship.

Having left Plymouth some two years earlier, our meetings, although random, never wavered in quality. It was always a pleasure, for both of us to meet up and chat. It never stopped being a relationship, a friendship. Yes, however infrequently we met, our friendship remained… frequent!

Then, one evening, I did just that. I infrequently turned up! I'd been selling The Issue in Penzance and arranged to return to Plymouth for a night out with Adam. Adam, by this time, was no longer a Big Issue vendor. And now, although having moved in with his partner, life for Adam was as homeless, fast and furious as it had ever been. Adam always needed more than he had, more than existed.

I hadn't seen him for six months. We had a lot to catch up on. We took a slow, memorable walk to the local. Then, just before reaching the pub, Adam said the immortal words: "Hang on here mate, I just need to see somebody." Of course, I knew who that somebody was. And, of course, he knew that I knew who that somebody was. That somebody was a heroin dealer. Yes, Adam lived life in the fast lane. And whilst Adam was not a fully paid-up member of the heroin club, he did 'enjoy', he did need the random, occasional fix. The random dig.

As I stood on the corner waiting for Adam to return, unbeknown to me, Adam was lying prone on the carpet of his dealer's flat, dying. It was a bad hit! Of course, he may not have died had his dealer phoned the ambulance immediately. But his dealer's priority was money, heroin. So, whilst Adam was vulnerable, being stripped of his life, he was also being stripped of his watch, his money, even his jeans. Whilst, 100 yards away, I stood on the corner, waiting for my friend, my pal, to return for a drink, for a yarn.

Three weeks later, the dealer himself died from an overdose.

Yes, we often read in the papers of some youngster overdosing on heroin or see for ourselves a drunk on the streets. Many, I'm sure, will make some kind of judgement on these people or maybe even condemn. Yet all we see is one single snapshot of their lives. We know nothing else about them or their background to pass judgement and certainly not enough to condemn.

Another friend, who, through 'circumstances', struggled with life, was Graham 'Two Ties'. Graham, 48, who used to sell The Issue, had spent most of his adult life on the streets. He was a man who, through his own admission, led a life of serious drug and alcohol abuse. Without describing Graham, that stand-alone statement would sound awfully shallow and one-dimensional.

Graham was an absolute spirit, a gentleman. Very aware, very astute. But he cared too much. It seems strange to preface the phrase 'cared too much' with 'but', but that's how it was. On a practical level, he cared about people. As a Big Issue vendor, he would never pass a beggar without giving them a share of his money. On a spiritual level, he cared about, and became distressed at, all that was wrong with the world. Injustice, greed, poverty.

Alcohol and drugs were, for Graham, a release that gave him the capacity to relax, the capacity for a while to stop worrying. Unfortunately, over the years, that 'release' took control both mentally and physically, but Graham's spirit remained intact.

After many years on the streets, roaming from town to town, Graham landed in Plymouth and started selling the Big Issue. The rewards this offered, not just financial, but in meeting people and developing friendships, gave Graham the impetus he needed. Within months, Graham was off the streets into a flat. For him, a huge achievement. He was suddenly enthused. He bought two snakes who became his family and, more importantly, it gave him the responsibility of looking after them. A responsibility he undertook with a passion. He made friends and slowly became integrated into his local community.

Although still indulging in the occasional drinking binge, these were undertaken in a very much controlled environment. He now had responsibilities, a job, a home, friends, a life! As if to underline that fact, Graham would sometimes pack a bag and sleep rough for the night in what I believe was, like his occasional binges, a controlled step backward to enable him to see how far he'd moved forward. To put into perspective how much he'd achieved.

The last time I saw Graham was December 19th, 2003. We were both visiting mutual friends of ours, Kev 'the Hat' and his teenage son. Kev, being the perfect host, ensured a nice relaxed evening, helped along with a few drinks, Kev's guitar and, as we hadn't seen each other for a while, lots of news to catch up on.

At 10pm, Graham decided to go home as he had to feed his snakes and get up early the following morning. "You'll have to come down and see my flat," said Graham, "I've changed all the furniture around, it looks really cool." I promised to visit the following week. We all said our goodbyes and Graham left.

At 3.30am, asleep on Kev's sofa, I was awakened by someone shouting and pounding on Kev's door. Fumbling in the dark, I managed to open the door to be met by a resident from the flat below. Pointing down the stairs, he yelled, "it's your friend! It's your friend!" What was he on about? I walked out onto the landing and there, at the foot of the stairs, was Graham. Rushing to him, I immediately saw there was no urgency. Graham was very obviously dead.

The police and C.I.D. arrived and went about their business. After questioning us, they interviewed the residents in the adjoining flats. We just sat there. Numb. I think with the death of anyone who's a part of your life, it's surreal, impossible to comprehend the finality. We just sat there, not speaking a word.

A constable interrupted us, "have you got an old blanket we can chuck over your mate?" Numb, we just accepted everything that was happening. In retrospect, "an old blanket to chuck over your mate?" "What, an old blanket to chuck over our friend who's just died?" "No! Give him the best fuckin' blanket in the house." But we were numb. We just accepted everything that was happening. We even accepted that, rather than taking Graham away first, we, including Kev's teenage son, were made to clamber past his body to go to the station for further investigation.

We arrived at the station, were questioned for an hour and had our clothes seized for forensics. Apparently, until proven otherwise, Graham's death was being treated as suspicious.

It was light when we returned to the flat. The police had left and Graham's body had been taken away. With Graham gone, it was even harder to comprehend, to grasp the reality of what had happened. Entering the flat, it was shrouded, as we were, with a cold, eerie silence. We just sat there, once again. Numb. After a couple of hours, with hardly a word spoken, I decided to drive back to my pitch in Yeovil. I needed some space. I wished Kev and his son well, and in turn Kev promised to keep me informed.

Two days before Christmas I read in the newspaper that following an autopsy, Graham's death had now been confirmed as an accident. We heard nothing from the police.

After spending Christmas day alone in my lay-by near Yeovil, I suddenly had an overwhelming need for companionship, succour. My silent plea was answered almost immediately. I received a 'phone call from a customer, a friend, wishing me a happy Christmas. I told her what had happened and she immediately invited me to stay with her for a while, in Paignton. I accepted her offer, thanked her and left immediately.

For the next week, my friend insisted on tending my every need, whilst I simply wallowed, immersing myself in her kindness. For the first time since Graham had died, my head was clear, I could think straight, I felt stronger.

The coroner's office 'phoned to inform me that the funeral would take place the following week. Almost immediately, I received another 'phone call; it was the vicar who was conducting the service. He wanted to meet Kev and me to talk about Graham's life and discuss the order of service. "Shouldn't you be asking his family?" I enquired. "I know Graham had little contact with his family over the years, but the little he spoke about his past revealed that he did have a mother, a brother and a number of children." "The police can't find any next of kin," he replied. I was shocked, saddened.

With only two days left before the funeral, we met the vicar. He was an amiable young man who listened intently to our recollection of Graham. For me, it was quite cathartic, talking about Graham's life to a complete stranger. Turning a name into a person. After the meeting, I arranged to give Kev a lift to the funeral. We talked about Graham's family and he too was convinced his mother was still alive and felt sure he had some children. He too was saddened that they couldn't be found. Driving back to Paignton, this haunted me.

On arriving back, I immediately phoned the police, the first contact I'd had with them since the death. After being directed to the relevant department, I asked what enquiries they had made in trying to locate Graham's family. They informed me that 'extensive investigations' were carried out but now that the death was being treated as an accident, the file had been sent to the coroner's office. It was now their duty to find the next of kin. I thanked them for their help and hung up. I'd initially had this bizarre idea that I alone could maybe locate Graham's family. After my call to the police, I realised that if they and the coroner's office couldn't come up with anything, what chance did I have? But I felt uneasy. There was something not quite right. I mulled over the past events. Then I realised where my unease lay. The police!

When Graham's death went from being suspicious to accidental, I would have thought it a standard procedure, if not a required courtesy, to inform those deemed under suspicion, that they were no longer so. We'd heard nothing. Then there were the 'extensive investigations' to find the next of kin. Two principal lines of enquiry surely would have been his friends and his place of work, The Big Issue. But not a call to either! I phoned the police again to voice my concerns. They referred me to the coroner. I phoned the coroner, it was Sunday, nobody could help me.

I was angry, frustrated. I needed to do something. I needed to find Graham's family.

My friend suggested that, with so little time left, I should look on the internet. I knew Graham's surname was Fisher and that he was born in the Leicester area. Armed only with this information, I tentatively entered cyberspace. Within five minutes, I had a printed list of 157 Fishers in the Leicester area, complete with telephone numbers. Wow! I studied the list for what seemed an age, 157 names, perhaps 157 families enjoying their day. Going for an afternoon walk, enjoying lunch, playing with the children, perhaps one family thinking about their son, brother, father: Graham, whom they hadn't heard from in years.

My friend poured me a very stiff drink. I started dialling. My enquiry had to be polite but succinct. Time was not on my side. The first person to answer was obviously of eastern origin. "Hello," I said, "I'm looking for relatives of Graham Fisher, aged 47 and lived most of his life on the streets." "You have to ask husband, he is the Fisher in family, you ring later," she replied. One down, 156 to go. The next two conversations were with answering machines. The next call was a negative. I realised this could be a long night. On to the next. "Hello, I'm looking for relatives of Graham Fisher, aged 47 and lived most of his life on the streets." "Oh, that'll be my cousin," the voice said. I was stunned. This was only the third person I'd spoken to. It couldn't be this easy. Gathering myself, I realised I had to be absolutely sure we were both talking about the same man before I delivered my news. After a few telling questions, it was obvious I'd found Graham's family. In the next half an hour, I spoke to Graham's mum, sister and brother. The funeral was cancelled for a week whilst the family organised their trip to Plymouth. After our conversation, I was overcome with a spectrum of emotions. Thrilled at having found his family, sad that I had to inform them of his death and so very angry that what took me, a domestic computer and ten minutes to accomplish, couldn't be achieved by the police, the coroner and a wealth of resources in three weeks.

The following day, Graham's brother rang to inform me that he'd contacted the coroner and the funeral was now arranged for the following week. The very next day, the coroner's office phoned to inform me of the change in the funeral arrangements because, "we've managed to locate Mr Fisher's relatives". I hung up, not saying a word. The following week, the night before Graham's funeral, Kev and I met Graham's family at a nearby hotel. There was Graham's mum, brother, sister and one of his four children. We were asked about Graham's last years. We told them of Graham's achievements, his flat, his snakes. We told them how he'd taken control of his life. How proud he was and indeed how proud they should be of him. They listened intently. Graham's brother Derek, who acted as sort of spokesman, was very friendly and receptive. This surprised me. Whenever Graham had talked about his brother, it was always with a kind of resentment. Yet this guy was obviously distressed at losing Graham, obviously cared deeply. Something didn't quite fit. We carried on talking. As I was informing them about what little effort the police had made in trying to locate his family, a large man bounded into the room, walked over to us and before sitting down, stated, "why the fuck should the police make any effort? He never did them any favours. He was a fuckin' druggie!" I was introduced to Graham's other brother. We didn't shake hands. Kev and I said goodbye to the family and left.

There was a good crowd at the funeral. Friends and Big Issue customers and, of course, Graham's family. After the service, Derek thanked me for everything and told me that had the police searched his brother's flat they would have found a pile of paperwork on the table. The document at the top of that pile was Graham's birth certificate. On it was an address that would have led them directly to his mother.

Now this is not a condemnation of the police in general. My address book contains many telephone numbers and addresses of people I've met on the way, all very good friends, from all walks of life, including some, who happen to be in the police force. No, this is more a criticism of individuals. The police officer's thoughts, I'm sure, were one dimensional. They saw one snapshot of Graham's life. On that, they made a judgement. Perhaps condemned. This, I believe, manifested itself in the acute lack of effort in finding Graham's family and the contempt shown to his friends.

Graham Fisher had struggled with life. An alcoholic, Big Issue seller. Why should we make the effort? Why? Because both physically and spiritually he gave. Why? Because Graham was a human being. Why? Because this guy worried more than anyone should ever have to worry. Maybe he cared so much that it gave others the opportunity not to.

SO MANY FRIENDS

(FOR MYLES, GRAHAM TWO TIES, GEORDIE JOHN, PONTOON STEVE, TERESA, ADAM, AND FLUFFY MARK)

Don't place plastic flowers on my grave.
They tell me you're not coming back.

Bring me fresh roses whilst I'm able to smell
We could go for a walk, maybe talk some as well
And the fragrance of blossom and friendship combined,
Would beat plastic flowers of whatever kind.

Don't place plastic flowers on my grave.

Don't shed tears of grief at my graveside
Tears perhaps, tinged with regret

Pay me a visit whilst I too can cry
We could ignite some memories before it's goodbye
Where the only tears shed would be tears of delight
When banter and laughter might conquer the night

Don't shed tears of grief at my grave

Don't wear that black suit at my funeral
It's starting to look a touch frayed

Call round today, we could paint the town red
Burn the candle, both ends. Silly hats on our head
We could act just like kids and fair skip down the street
And make out we've still got the world at our feet

Don't wear that black suit at my grave

So just look at how many now stand here
Never knew I had so many friends

But why didn't you call
Whilst I could laugh, whilst I could think
Whilst I could join in a chat and a drink
Whilst I could listen, whilst I could smell
And whilst I could too, share the memories as well
Why didn't you call

Don't place plastic flowers on my grave
They tell me you're not coming back

I said goodbye to my friends. I needed to visit Bristol to see my children.

Now for sanity's sake, my trips to Bristol are infrequent. My life has in general, been a game of two halves. My children aside, the first half providing the injuries, the second half the goals. Every time I visit Bristol, I revisit the physical, visual and emotional reminders of a past that provided more pain than pleasure. I always arrive with the same eager anticipation, eager to see my children, catch up with old friends and visit family. But when I leave, I always leave floored. Emotionally wasted. To the point that, more often than not, I lock myself away in my van for a few days till my head eases sufficiently to allow me once again, to 'be'.

This latest trip was no different. It was my son's 24th birthday which, not only coincides with my wedding anniversary but also with the anniversary of the death of his only cousin, Darren.

Arriving mid-evening, I spent a couple of hours with old friends, watching home videos from yesteryear, yesterlife. The following morning, as arranged, I visited my 14-year-old daughter Leanne; she talked about her plans for the future. "First I'm going to college Dad, then university to try for a degree in sports science." Was I Mr Proud? An hour later my son Andrew arrived. He hadn't seen his sister in more than six months. They had lots to catch up on; I decided to leave them to it. I gave Andrew his present and suggested it must be a burden that his birthday was also the anniversary of his cousin's death. "No Dad," he replied. "It reminds me how lucky I am. I loved him Dad. That can never be a burden." Mr Proud again. I, at that moment, realised how lucky I was. Even with the difficult childhoods that both Leanne and Andrew had been dealt, the legacy of damage I witness, day in, day out, being handed down from one generation to the next, had all but vanished.

I called round to see my sister. We, for the first time, didn't mention Darren. She was surprisingly cool. Gone was the overwhelming grief that had enveloped her for the past five years. She also talked to me with a respect I hadn't witnessed for a long time, recalling events from our childhood. "Remember when you were about seven and I was six. I had a badly infected finger and you were sent home from school because you had impetigo, a skin infection. Our Mum wouldn't take us to the hospital so we walked there and got treated ourselves." I didn't remember.

After I'd left, I sat alone in the pub for a while, thinking of what she'd told me. I couldn't think of myself as a seven year old. It was so long ago. So I imagined these random children walking hand in hand to the hospital, afraid and alone. How sad. Then, slowly, imagination turned into stark, vivid reality. That random little boy became me. I was back there with Gill, once again sat side by side in the treatment room. Gill having her fingernail removed, me having the scabs peeled from my face. Holding hands, both crying, not over our own pain, but each others'. Reliving the experience felt infinitely more painful than the experience itself. This was something I didn't need to remember. This was one of many memories I'd buried long ago. Sunken with its well-fitting concrete boot. But a memory that now, I'll never forget.

I didn't, as arranged, get to see my brother that evening. I was ninety miles away, parked in my van, alone with one sad head and sixty unsold Issues.

THE BIG
ISSUE

NO CHANGE GIVEN.
CHANGE COMES
FROM WITHIN

Chapter 8
Out of the blue
[AS IT HAPPENED]

SCENE:

Sunday afternoon. A dreary, overcast day. Graham, small-town, mild-mannered, Big Issue man, has lots of Issues left. Needs to shift them today. Decides to travel to Plymouth metropolis. To induce a feeling of nostalgia, he pitches up on the pavement outside Boots the chemist, his first ever pitch. Graham sets up sign, 'PLEASE QUEUE IN AN ORDERLY FASHION.' He places mock Big Issue CCTV on his head, made out of a shoebox and a polystyrene cup, and awaits his first sale.

Enter right: Burly Boots security guard.

BURLY BOOTS SECURITY GUARD (brutish) *"Oy! You can't stand by that wall there. You gotta stand by that wall there!"*

Small-town Big Issue man obliges and nudges along to next wall.

BURLY BOOTS SECURITY GUARD *"And while we're about it, what's yer name?"*

MILD-MANNERED BIG ISSUE MAN *"I'm sorry?"*

BURLY BOOTS SECURITY GUARD (brutish x2) *"I said what's yer name?"*

MILD-MANNERED BIG ISSUE MAN (confused) *"Why on earth should I give you my name?"*

BURLY BOOTS SECURITY GUARD (semi officious/pseudo-intelligent) *"It's all part of the Plymouth City Centre initiative to clear the streets of beggars and undesirables. I'm allowed to ask yer name."*

MILD-MANNERED BIG ISSUE MAN *"Well you've asked, now I'm sorry but if you don't mind I have Big Issues to deal with."*

BURLY BOOTS SECURITY GUARD (I'm losin' my cool/gonna sort you) *"If you don't gimme yer name I'm gonna phone yer boss."*

MILD-MANNERED BIG ISSUE MAN *"The manager is in France for two weeks."*

(Pause)

BURLY BOOTS SECURITY GUARD *"Ahh, we got a hotline to ring if vendors are out of order."*

MILD-MANNERED BIG ISSUE MAN (Defeated) *"OK, OK it's Harry."*

BURLY BOOTS SECURITY GUARD *"Arry what?*

MILD-MANNERED BIG ISSUE MAN *"Houdini."*

BURLY BOOTS SECURITY GUARD *"Are you sure?"*

MILD-MANNERED BIG ISSUE MAN (offended) *"Are you calling me a liar?"*

Burly Boots security guard scribbles down name. Exits.

Small-town Big Issue man loses zest for working. Takes off badge, packs up pitch and starts striding out of Plymouth metropolis.

Police patrol vehicle, two occupants, approaches from behind. Vehicle stops. Passenger winds down window.

CONSTABLE No.1 *"Afternoon."*

MILD-MANNERED BIG ISSUE MAN *"Afternoon constable."*

CONSTABLE No.1 *"Have you just been selling the Big Issue?"*

MILD MANNERED BIG ISSUE MAN *"Don't tell me, you've had a call from the Burly Boots security guard."*

CONSTABLE No.1 *"No we've had a call from the C.C.T.V. control room to check out a male, Caucasian, Big Issue vendor with a C.C.T.V. on his head*.*"*

CONSTABLE No.2 *"Yeah, what's it all about?"*

MILD MANNERED BIG ISSUE MAN *"Sorry. What's what all about?"*

CONSTABLE No.2 (frustrated) *"The C.C.T.V. on your head."*

MILD MANNERED BIG ISSUE MAN *"It's a joke officer. It's an irony. It's a cardboard box and a polystyrene cup."*

CONSTABLE No.2 (confused) *"Ah, I see. Right, the other thing is why are you dressed in such an eccentric manner, orange scarf, tartan trousers and the like"?*

MILD MANNERED BIG ISSUE MAN *"So you've stopped me today because I've got a cardboard box on my head and in your eyes I'm not quite colour co-ordinated."*

CONSTABLE No.1 *"We're just checking you out sir."*

Officer takes small town Big Issue man's name and date of birth.

CONSTABLE No.1 *"Well that's all thank you. Are you planning to sell again in Plymouth?"*

Small town Big Issue man… vacates!

Chapter 9
Outlook bright

O n occasion, I'm invited to speak at local secondary schools. It's always an absolute honour to have the opportunity to share my experiences and to perhaps dispel preconceived views the children may have about the homeless. Preconceived views that are often delivered as fact.

I always introduce my talk with a story about The Prof who I'd met in Devon some ten years ago. The Prof was homeless, clothes caked with vomit and urine. He would often be seen sitting in the town centre with a bottle glued to his lips. I would ask the children for some words to describe him. The replies being predictable words such as 'scum', 'tramp', 'waster', 'disgusting'.

At the end of my talk, I always return to The Prof and explain a bit about his background, providing the children with a little knowledge that may enable them to make a more informed judgement. I would explain how, five years earlier, The Prof had been an academic, a teacher. Explain how one evening, when his young wife and baby were travelling to pick him up from work, both were killed in a road accident. Explain how The Prof, to blot out his pain, turned to drink. Explain how his life spiralled out of control. And how, years later, he ended up on the streets, a tramp, an alcoholic, sat on a town centre bench in Devon. Their now 'informed' responses are, for me, always the most rewarding of experiences.

After one of my talks, the teacher asked if I could stay behind as one of the pupils wanted to ask me a question in private. I agreed. The classroom then emptied leaving myself, the teacher and a young girl. I'd noticed the girl on a few occasions during my talk. During the question and answer session at the end, she seemed agitated, as though desperately wanting to speak but desperately suppressing what she wanted to say. With her schoolmates now gone, she could hold back no longer. She immediately burst into tears, sobbing uncontrollably. Her teacher tried to pacify her whilst I, for no other reason than witnessing her upset, burst into tears myself. The teacher, after successfully calming us both down, gently prompted the young girl to speak. The girl told me that her father too was an alcoholic. Her father, who she hadn't seen in over 18 months, in February had been found dead in his room at a hostel for the homeless. The girl and her mother had gone to the hostel to pick up his belongings and found in one of his drawers, Christmas presents and a letter to her. She recalled to me some of the wonderful memories she had of him and how much she desperately missed him. She then read me his letter. It was now my turn to instigate the sobbing. I sobbed, the young girl sobbed, even the teacher couldn't hold back this time. This poor child had no question to ask. She simply wanted someone to talk to. Someone who'd been there and could perhaps understand. Maybe I was the closest she could now ever get to her father. And indeed, perhaps her talk was not necessarily to me, but to him.

Knowles-Hill School,
Old Exter Road
Newton Abbout,
Devon
TQ12 2ns

Dear Mr Grahon,

Thank you for coming in to our school and showing us not to take the piss out of homless people and we now Realise that homeless people are there for a Reuson and not there just because they want to lounge around be Lazy and clame on benfits Thankyou again!

Yours Sincerely

David Jones

Knowlesh Hill School
Old Exeter Road,
Newton Abbot
Devon

1st November 2001

Dear Graham,
Thank you for coming in to our less[on]
and telling us about what it is like to have ho[me]
and telling us about your family,
It has made me realise how alone it must be and [...]
people leave home.
You have persuaded me not to leave home because of
the drugs and deaths on the streets.

Yours Sincerely,

Darren Preece.

SORRY TO HEAR YOU ARE LEAVING NEWTON ABBOT
— THANK YOU FOR YOUR WIT & HUMOUR, YOU
HAVE HELPED TO MAKE 1999 BEARABLE!

Hope you find lots of
success and happiness in
your new town. You will
be greatly missed by
Barnstaple.
All the best,
from
Lucy, Glyn and Patrick
Allen
xxx

You have been an
inspiration to me and I
will miss you. Jan

Graham

Happy Christmas

Thank you for making
Taunton a better place
+ for brightening our
day.

Philippa +
Alex.

Well done Graham for another year
to be proud of! Thanks for bringing
your talents and gifts to Totnes —
you've been such a blessing to the town
and so many people!
All the best for your future and
I'm looking forward to reading your
book!

All Best Wishes for your future.
Barnstaple won't be the
same without you

Amanda & Helen

Totnes will have lost
some of its sparkle when
you have moved on,
peace, love and light
Karen.

We will miss you.
Hope you come
back at some point.

Lovely to have known you

Take care of
yourself.

Fran, Mike, Freddie
Gregory Archie & Daisy
— x —

Thanking you for your generous
donation to our families this
Christmas, we wish you a very, very
happy Christmas
from all at South Devon Womens
Aid

Thanks for selling the Big Issue in
our little town and for all the
money you've raised too.
Good luck on your travels
love from Poppy & Annie xxx

Doreen + Philip Deslam

Dear Graham,
We would like to say, how much
you will be missed, when you leave Barnstaple,
your letters, enclosed with the Big Issue have
been a joy to read (I have kept them all) +
your work for the children, has been wonderful
We wish you all the luck in the world, in
your next abode, please accept the small
gift enclosed, with our love + best wishes.
Doreen + Philip.

P.S. Hope our next Big Issue seller, will be
as nice as you have been.

Graham.
We would like to thank you
for all that you've done for
others this year. God Bless
We will miss our little chat
and would like to wish ya
all the best for the
"New Year" 2001.
Hope to see you again
sometime Be lucky. and
keep warm + healthy.
Anne + Ron Pickarby.

To Graham
Many thanks for all that you're
done for Totnes. Wherever you roam
you will always have a home here.

With Best Wishes
for Christmas
and the New Year

with Love
Isabel x